Mastering Swift

An Introduction to Swift Scripting and Programming for Apple Admins

Charles Edge
Joel Rennich
Jeremy Bannister

Apress®

Mastering Swift: An Introduction to Swift Scripting and Programming for Apple Admins

Charles Edge
Minneapolis, MN, USA

Joel Rennich
Stillwater, MN, USA

Jeremy Bannister
New York, NY, USA

ISBN-13 (pbk): 979-8-8688-2769-3
ISBN-13 (electronic): 979-8-8688-2770-9
https://doi.org/10.1007/979-8-8688-2770-9

Managing Director, Apress Media LLC: Welmoed Spahr
Acquisitions Editor: Miriam Haidara
Editorial Assistant: Marina Engler

Cover designed by eStudioCalamar

Cover image designed by kjpargeter on Freepik.

Distributed to the book trade worldwide by Springer Science+Business Media New York, 1 New York Plaza, New York, NY 10004. Phone 1-800-SPRINGER, fax (201) 348-4505, e-mail orders-ny@springer-sbm.com, or visit www.springeronline.com. Apress Media, LLC is a Delaware LLC and the sole member (owner) is Springer Science + Business Media Finance Inc (SSBM Finance Inc). SSBM Finance Inc is a **Delaware** corporation.

For information on translations, please e-mail booktranslations@springernature.com; for reprint, paperback, or audio rights, please e-mail bookpermissions@springernature.com.

Apress titles may be purchased in bulk for academic, corporate, or promotional use. eBook versions and licenses are also available for most titles. For more information, reference our Print and eBook Bulk Sales web page at http://www.apress.com/bulk-sales.

Any source code or other supplementary material referenced by the author in this book is available to readers on GitHub. For more detailed information, please visit https://www.apress.com/gp/services/source-code.

If disposing of this product, please recycle the paper

I was blessed to meet Charles. He posted a job offer in 2021 – prototyping a password manager with an extra, somewhat unique layer of security, written in Swift – and I reached out to him. He was warm and colorful from the first phone call we had, and he seemed to like me too, because we decided to work together on the project called Secret Chest. I had the privilege of talking with Charles almost every day from the start of 2022 until he suddenly passed away in April of 2024. Our calls were full of enthusiasm. My enthusiasm about the cleanliness of some new piece of code, or about an advancement in the architecture of our test suite, or about a new analogy I had come up with. His enthusiasm about his latest 3D-printed creation, or about his kids, or about this book. And our mutual enthusiasm for each other's enthusiasm. I'm very happy to have had the chance to proofread Charles' manuscript and help his final work be enjoyed by his readers. In my world, Charles lives on not only in memory but also in name, because the same week that he passed away, my wife and I adopted a new little dog, and we decided to name him Charles (nicknamed "Charly").

With much love,
Jeremy

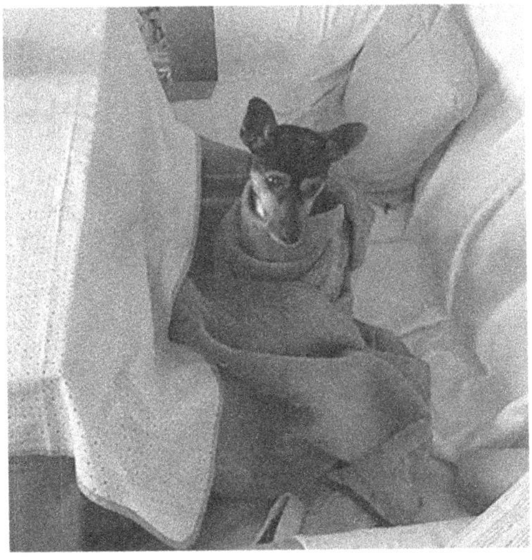

My dog Charles a.k.a. Charly

Table of Contents

About the Authors

Charles Edge was the CTO of bootstrappers.mn, the CTO/COO of secretchest.io, and a former director at Jamf where he led the development of Jamf Now. He held 35 years of experience as a developer, administrator, architect, product manager, entrepreneur, and CTO. He authored 25 books and more than 6,000 blog posts on technology and served as an editor and author for a number of publications. Charles served on the board of directors for a number of companies and nonprofits and frequently spoke at conferences including DefCon, BlackHat, LinuxWorld, the Apple Worldwide Developers Conference, and a number of Apple-focused conferences. Charles also authored krypted.com and was a cofounder/host of the MacAdmins Podcast and The History of Computing podcast. He passed away in April of 2024, and his extensive network of people felt the loss very deeply.

Joel Rennich is the SVP of Product at JumpCloud residing in the greater Minneapolis, MN, area. While Joel has spent most of his professional career focused on Apple products, at JumpCloud, he works with a team focused on boldly going where no devs have gone before across all platforms. Prior to JumpCloud, Joel was a director at Jamf helping to make Jamf Connect and other authentication products. In 2018, Jamf acquired Joel's startup, Orchard & Grove, which is where Joel developed the widely used open source software NoMAD. Installed on over one million Macs across the globe, NoMAD allowed macOS users to get all the benefits of Active Directory without having to be bound to them. Joel also developed other open source software at Orchard & Grove such as DEPNotify and NoMAD Login. Over the years, Joel has been a frequent speaker at a number of conferences including WWDC, MacSysAdmin, MacADUK, Penn State MacAdmins Conference, Objective by the Sea, FIDO, Authenticate, and others in addition to user groups everywhere. Joel spent over a decade working at Apple in Enterprise Sales and started the website `www.afp548.com`, which was the mainstay of Apple system administrator education during the early years of macOS X. Joel is a classically trained journalist and plied his trade as a paparazzi chasing Monica Lewinsky before rising to become the Director of Photography for United Press International in Washington DC. If you're lucky, he'll even tell you some of his Monica stories, as the stories are better than the photos.

Jeremy Bannister is a Swift developer from New York who now lives in Spain. He connected with Charles Edge in December of 2021 and began working for Charles to prototype a password management tool with a focus on resisting quantum computing decryption attacks. They worked together until Charles' unexpected passing in April 2024. Jeremy is happy to have helped proofread Charles' manuscript and helped to allow his final book to be published.

About the Technical Reviewer

Massimo Nardone has more than 30 years of experience in information and cybersecurity for IT/OT/IoT/IIoT, web/mobile development, cloud, and IT architecture. His true IT passions are security and Android. He holds an M.Sc. degree in computing science from the University of Salerno, Italy.

Throughout his working career, he has held various positions starting as programming developer, then security teacher, PCI QSA, auditor, assessor, lead IT/OT/SCADA/cloud architect, CISO, BISO, executive, program director, OT/IoT/IIoT security competence leader, etc. In his last working engagement, he worked as a seasoned cyber and information security executive, CISO, and OT, IoT, and IIoT security competence leader, helping many clients to develop and implement cyber, information, OT, and IoT security activities.

He is currently working as Vice President of OT Security for SSH Communications Security.

He is a co-author of numerous Apress books, including *Spring Security 6 Recipes, Secure RESTful APIs, Cybersecurity Threats and Attacks in the Gaming Industry, Pro Spring Security, Beginning EJB in Java EE 8, Pro JPA 2 in Java EE 8,* and *Pro Android Games,* and has reviewed more than 100 titles.

CHAPTER 1

SwiftUI

Systems administrators often need to present simple user interfaces to aid users in providing information or taking actions. This might be to elevate privileges from within some kind of self-service portal, to force restarts based on complicated logic, or just to show a user what's happening on their computer during administrative routines. Once upon a time, that might have been AppleScript or some kind of graphical interface from a third party. Today, those types of tasks should almost exclusively be handled by SwiftUI.

SwiftUI is a modern framework used to build user interfaces for Apple platforms. It is a declarative framework, which means developers tell SwiftUI what the user interface should look like, and SwiftUI, in a way, figures out how to make it happen. This is a very different approach from previous versions of interface languages for Apple, where complicated design patterns to connect buttons to functions were required. In fact, SwiftUI often feels more similar to modern web design techniques, where the logic for the interface is completely separate from the back-end code (e.g., HTML as a front-end for JavaScript or Python).

There are other options for interface design, like Objective-C options and UIKit or AppKit. UIKit is part of the Cocoa Touch layer on iOS, which is the graphical user interface (GUI) layer of the operating system, and AppKit is the equivalent for macOS. But we'll stick primarily with SwiftUI in this book. A few other reasons to consider SwiftUI:

- **Declarative**: As mentioned, SwiftUI is a declarative framework, which makes it easy to create complex user interfaces.
- **Easy to learn**: SwiftUI is an easy framework to learn. Web developers will find the declarative layout similar in some ways to CSS.

C. Edge et al., *Mastering Swift*, https://doi.org/10.1007/979-8-8688-2770-9_1

- **Cross-platform**: SwiftUI can be used to create user interfaces for all Apple platforms, including iOS, iPadOS, macOS, tvOS, and watchOS. This means many users might, for example, use one app with different views to deliver apps for iPhone, iPad, and Mac.
- **Fast**: SwiftUI is a fast framework. User interfaces will be responsive and smooth, even on older devices (unless Xcode says otherwise). One reason it's fast is that it's fairly lightweight, unlike some tools that allow developers to "write once, run anywhere" where there's a lot of cruft that might be hundreds of megabytes larger and slower than the same app that was built in native Swift.

While SwiftUI is more iOS-focused, it's still the easiest way to get started on developing a UI on Mac.

Ultimately, it shouldn't be hard to convince anyone to use SwiftUI; it's basically the default way to build interfaces in apps (although there are other libraries, many of which existed before Apple released SwiftUI). Apple has also made it very clear that SwiftUI is the future for UI development on any Apple platform.

Basic SwiftUI Use

SwiftUI is fairly easy to pick up, even for people who have no background in programming. Having said that, a background in programming will of course help! Terms and concepts are unique to SwiftUI though, so it helps to understand a few basic concepts. These include

- **Views**: Views are the building blocks of SwiftUI user interfaces to display content and handle user interactions. We'll begin with a single-view app in this chapter, but it's possible to have a number of different views as end users navigate through an application and the usefulness of the app increases.
- **Modifiers**: Modifiers are used to customize the appearance and behavior of views. They can change the size, color, font, and other properties of views.

- **Bindings**: Bindings connect views to data sources, to update the appearance of a view based on the value of a data source, for example, if a user has not configured a username or password, provided an entitlement so an app can access a specific type of functionality, or is in a different physical location.
- **State**: State is used to store the values of variables that change over time, such as the current value of a text field or the selected item in a list.

We can then dig a little deeper into each of the above elements, beginning with the different types of views made available in SwiftUI:

- **Text:** Views that display text.
- **Image:** Views that display images.
- **Button:** Views that respond to user taps.
- **Label:** Views that display labels.
- **Form:** Views that contain other views.
- **Modifiers:** Modifiers customize the appearance and behavior of views. They can be used to change the size, color, font, and other properties of views.

The above are the standard elements people are used to seeing in apps and can overlap or be rendered within one another, for example, a button with an image in it. Modifiers are functions that are called on views and which return modified versions of the view. For example, create a new project in Xcode and add the following code to create a button with a red background:

swift

```
Button(action: {
    // Do something when the button is tapped.
}) {
    Text("Button")
        .background(Color.red)
}
```

Figure 1-1 shows the resulting image, now with the button, on the right panel of the screen. This is made possible by the `#Preview` stanza of code automatically added to a `ContentView`, but which can be added to other SwiftUI files as well:

swift

```
#Preview {
    ContentView()
}
```

Figure 1-1. *Adding a* `Button`

Bindings are values of type `Binding`, and they're commonly created from state using the $ prefix. For example, the following code creates a text field that is bound to a variable called `name` (provided the variable was defined within the scope of the view):

swift

```
TextField("Your name", text: $name)
```

This code will update the text field whenever the value of the name variable changes. State is created using the `@State` property wrapper. For example, the following creates a variable called `name` that is stored in state:

swift

```
@State var name = ""
```

This variable can be updated by the user, and the changes will be reflected in the user interface as seen in Figure 1-2.

***Figure 1-2.** Adding a `TextField`*

Each of these are fairly simple, but it takes time to figure out when to use each and why – or at least beyond the academic definitions used thus far. However, combining elements is how nearly every app is built (although some don't use SwiftUI and use other frameworks, but that's beyond our scope for now). Since an application can be built just with SwiftUI (albeit a simplistic one), let's start with how to create a simple SwiftUI project.

Create a Simple SwiftUI Project

Swift is used to create massive projects by many of our favorite developers, but it's designed to be simple and offer a barrier of entry for new projects commensurate with what's being attempted. For our first project, to showcase SwiftUI, we'll create what's known as a Single `View` App, or an app with one view. This is done in Xcode, so we'll begin by creating a new project.

Creating a New Project in Xcode

To create a simple SwiftUI project in Xcode, follow these steps:

1. Open Xcode.
2. Click on File ➤ New ➤ Project.
3. In the Project Template window, select App and click Next.
4. Enter a name for your project and select a location to save it.
5. In the Choose options for your new project window, select the SwiftUI checkbox and click Next.
6. Click Create.

Once created, a `ContentView` file appears in the project navigator. This file contains the user interface for your app.

If you've built apps using UIKit or AppKit, you might be used to storyboards and view controllers. SwiftUI apps generally don't require storyboards at all; instead, you compose your interface out of `View` structs like `ContentView`.

Views are the building blocks of the user interface. They can be used to display text, images, buttons, and other elements. To add a SwiftUI view to your app, you can follow these steps:

Once created, here's how to add a SwiftUI view:

1. Right-click on the project navigator and select "New File."
2. Select the "Source" category and select the "SwiftUI `View`" template.
3. Enter a name for your view and click "Create."

4. The `ContentView` is then shown in the file list. Click to bring up the default `ContentView`:

5. Open it to see the following:

swift

```
import SwiftUI

struct ContentView: View {
    var body: some View {
        VStack {
            Image(systemName: "globe")
                .imageScale(.large)
                .foregroundStyle(.tint)
            Text("Krypted!")
        }
        .padding()
    }
}
#Preview {
    ContentView()
}
```

As can be seen in Figure 1-3, when highlighted, the `ContentView` displays automatically in the preview pane to the right of the code editor.

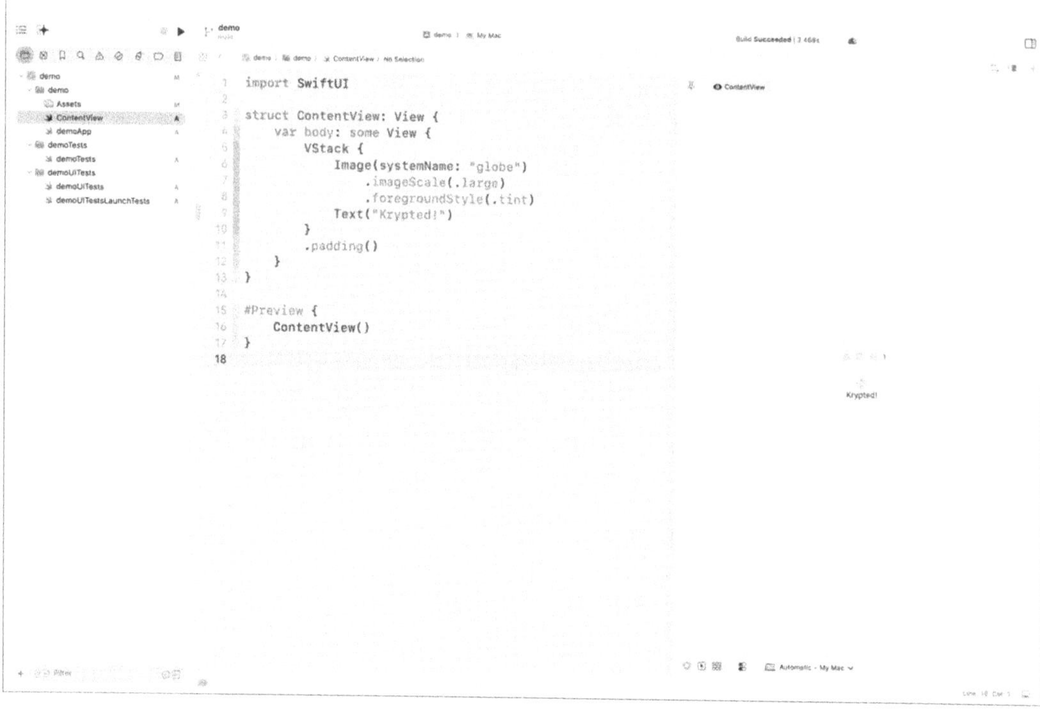

Figure 1-3. *SwiftUI Preview in Xcode*

This code creates a view that displays the text “Krypted!". We’ll get into struct and var later in the book, but for now, it’s good to know how to create a simple Hello World project ("Hello World!” was changed to “Krypted” for the lulz). To run your SwiftUI view, click the “Play” button in the top left corner of Xcode. The preview will stop and the view will be displayed in the simulator, as seen in Figure 1-4.

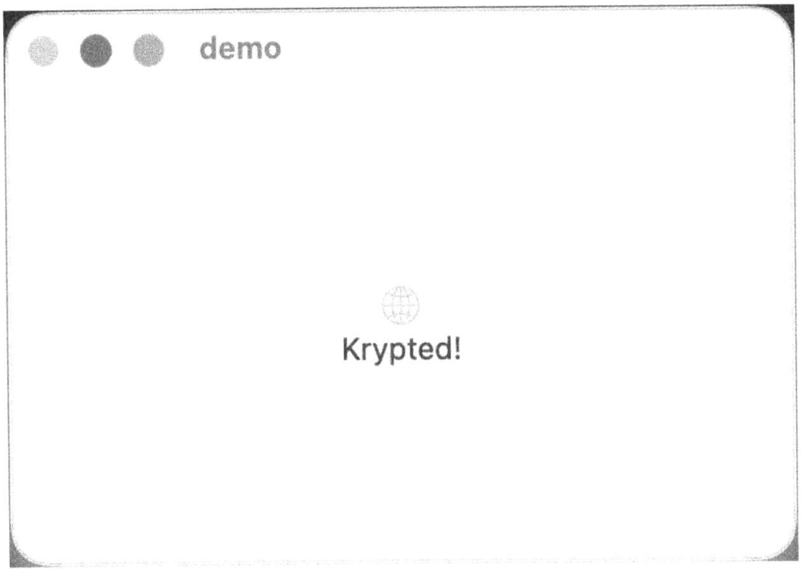

Figure 1-4. *The Test App*

The resultant app that was temporarily built isn't signed and notarized. We'll explain those concepts later in the book, but for now, just know that unsigned and unnotarized apps have limitations around distribution and can trigger additional security prompts depending on how they're launched. The build products are typically stored in `~/Library/Developer/Xcode/DerivedData`, where ~ refers to the home directory of the active logged in user.

Now that there is an app with a view, it's possible to do much more with them.

Understanding Views

SwiftUI views are the building blocks of SwiftUI user interfaces. They are responsible for displaying content and handling user interactions. Every custom view in SwiftUI conforms to the `View` protocol. The `View` protocol is a type that represents part of an app's user interface and provides modifiers that you use to configure views.

To recap the types of views:

- `Text`: Views that display text
- `Image`: Views that display images
- `Button`: Views that respond to user taps
- Label: Views that display labels
- `Form`: Views that contain other views

Views can be combined and nested to create complex user interfaces. For example, create a view that displays a list of items, each of which is a button that displays the item's name. Views are also highly customizable. Use modifiers to change the size, color, font, and other properties of views. For example, use a modifier to make a button red and another modifier to make it larger.

SwiftUI views are also declarative, which means that the code instructs SwiftUI as to how the user interface should look, and SwiftUI figures out how to make it happen. This makes SwiftUI views easy to use and maintain, although that's covered in later parts of the book.

Note Xcode can sometimes display prompts when it's unclear how to render elements on a screen.

Using Modifiers to Customize Views

Modifiers are used to change the size, color, font, and other properties of views. Modifiers can also be used to add interactivity to views. To use a modifier, you simply add it to a view. For example, the following code creates a button with a red background:

swift

```
Button(action: {
    // Do something when the button is tapped.
}) {
    Text("Button")
        .background(Color.red)
}
```

The .background() modifier renders whatever view you pass to it as the background of the view that you applied the modifier to. In this case, Color.red is the view that we passed as the argument, and therefore, the background will appear red. There are many different modifiers available in SwiftUI. You can find a list of all the available modifiers in the SwiftUI documentation at https://developer.apple.com/documentation/swiftui/viewmodifier.

Here are some of the most commonly used modifiers:

- font(): Changes the font of a view
- foregroundColor(): Changes the foreground color of a view
- padding(): Adds padding to a view
- border(): Adds a border to a view
- cornerRadius(): Rounds the corners of a view
- shadow(): Adds a shadow to a view

Modifiers can also be combined to create more complex effects. For example, the following code creates a button with a red background, a white border, and rounded corners:

swift

```
Button(action: {
    // Do something when the button is tapped.
}) {
     Text("Button")
         .background(Color.red)
         .border(Color.white, width: 2)
         .cornerRadius(10)
}
```

Modifiers help to create dynamic user interfaces, or those that aren't just the custom objects provided by Apple. They can create a beautiful or murky, ugly interface. To help stay pretty and useful, use the #Preview syntax as seen above to preview the changes to a view without having to run the app. This is similar to the original web design software packages like Hot Dog Pro.

Note Also experiment with the `.help()` modifier to add a help button to a view and the `.disabled()` modifier to disable a view.

Understanding Bindings

Bindings in SwiftUI connect the state of a view to the state of another view or to a value in your code. To understand bindings, it is important to understand the concept of state in SwiftUI. State is the data that changes over time in an app. For example, the text that a user enters into a text field is state.

Bindings connect the state of one view to the state of another view. For example, connect the text that a user enters into a text field to the title of a button. This way, the title of the button will always be updated to reflect the text that the user has entered. Bindings can also be used to connect the state of a view to a value. For example, connect the value of a stepper function to the value of a variable. This way, the value of the stepper will always be updated to reflect the value of the variable. Bindings can be a bit confusing at first, but make code more reactive and easier to understand.

How to Use Bindings to Connect Views

The `Binding` type is used to connect views. Most of the time, you create a binding by passing `$someStateValue` into a control. When you need to build a binding manually, you can do so using `Binding(get:set:)`. Here is an example of how to use bindings to connect views in SwiftUI:

swift

```
import SwiftUI
struct ContentView: View {
    @State private var name = ""
    var body: some View {
        VStack {
            TextField("Enter your name", text: $name)
            Text("Your name is \(name)")
        }
    }
}
```

This code will create a text field and a text view. The text field will be bound to the `name` property, which is a `@State` variable. This means that the text field will update `name` whenever the user enters text. The text view will display the current value of `name`.

When the user enters text into the text field, the name property will change. This will trigger the closure that is passed to the `Binding` struct. The closure will update the text view to reflect the new value of the name property.

Creating a Simple User Interface

One of the most important aspects of designing software for Apple devices is to create beautiful, sleek interfaces. Luckily, Apple made it hard not to build a great user interface as they are incorporating SwiftUI into all of their newer applications themselves. This has been in Apple's DNA for decades (for anyone who doubts that, just read *Enchantment* or *Art of the Start*, by Guy Kawasaki).

As we go through the options in this chapter and throughout the book, keep a few core ideas in mind:

- Start with a good design. The first step to building a beautiful user interface is to have a good design. This means having a clear idea of what the interface should look like and how it should function. There are a number of resources available to help you with this, such as the Human Interface Guidelines from Apple.
- Use colors and typography effectively. Colors and typography can have a big impact on the overall look and feel of an interface. Use them wisely to create a sense of harmony and balance.
- Use spacing and layout effectively. The way you space and layout your elements can have a big impact on the usability of your interface. Use spacing to create a sense of hierarchy and layout your elements in a way that is easy to understand and navigate. SwiftUI will naturally help here, especially on iOS to "do the right thing" a lot of times.
- Use animation and motion effectively. Animation and motion can be used to add interest and excitement to an interface. However, use them sparingly, and make sure they are used in a way that is meaningful and enhances the user experience.

- Test the interface. Once there's an interface, it is important to test it to make sure it is working as expected. This includes testing it on different devices, when code is in different states, and on devices with different screen sizes.

Another aspect to consider is just how much gets plopped onto each view. Less is more. If the app needs a lot of extra options, put them in a disclosure triangle or menu that opens up other options. Try to keep them less than a couple of clicks or taps away, but keep an eye on well-spaced elements and not too many. Most of us who have been systems administrators might think that the output for a bash command is a fine enough user interface; however, if we build tools with a graphical interface, we might as well make them look nice.

Creating a Button

`Button` is a SwiftUI view that allows users to interact with your app. It is a powerful tool that can be used to perform actions, navigate to different screens, and present alerts.

To create a button in SwiftUI, you can use the `Button` struct. The `Button` struct has a number of properties that you can use to customize the appearance and behavior of the button, such as the title, the background color, and the action that will be performed when the button is tapped. Here is an example of how to create a button in SwiftUI:

swift

```
import SwiftUI
struct ContentView: View {
    var body: some View {
        Button(
            "Click Me!",
            action: {
                print("Button was tapped!")
            }
        )
    }
}
```

This code will create a button with the title "Click Me!". The button will use the system's default styling (typically your app's accent/tint color). When the button is tapped, the `print()` function will be called, and the text "Button was tapped!" will be printed to the console.

The `Button` struct is a powerful tool that can be used to interact with your app. You can use the `Button` struct to create buttons with a variety of appearances and behaviors. Here are some additional tips for creating buttons in SwiftUI:

- Set the label text (or provide a custom label view) to control what's displayed on the button.
- Use modifiers like `.tint(...)`, `.buttonStyle(...)`, `.padding()`, and `.background(...)` to control appearance.
- Put work in the button's `action` closure to run code when tapped.

Buttons typically perform an action – we also usually have some text to explain what the button does.

Creating a Text Field

`TextField` is a SwiftUI view that allows users to enter text. It is a powerful tool that can be used to collect user input in your apps. To create a text field in SwiftUI, you can use the `TextField` struct. The `TextField` struct has a number of properties that you can use to customize the appearance and behavior of the text field, such as the placeholder text, the keyboard type, and the text editing behavior.

Here is an example of how to create a text field in SwiftUI:

swift

```
import SwiftUI
struct ContentView: View {
    @State private var name = ""
    var body: some View {
        TextField(
            "Enter your name",
            text: Binding(
                get: { self.name },
                set: { self.name = $0 }
            )
        )
    }
}
```

This code creates a text field with the placeholder text "Enter your name." The text field will be bound to the name property, which is a State variable. This means that the text field will update the name property whenever the user enters text into the text field.

Use the `TextField` struct to create text fields with a variety of appearances and behaviors. There are common properties and modifiers that can frequently be seen in projects. One is the keyboardType property to set the keyboard type that will be used in the text field. Another is the `textFieldStyle()` modifier, to change the way that the system styles that particular text field. In addition to a pure text field, there are other ways to display text - like a label.

Creating a Label

To create a label in SwiftUI, you can use the `Label` struct. The `Label` struct is a view that displays text along with an icon. Here is an example of how to create a label in SwiftUI:

swift

```
import SwiftUI
struct ContentView: View {
    var body: some View {
        Label(
            "Delete",
         systemImage: "trash.fill"
        )
    }
}
```

This code creates a label with the text "Delete" and with the built-in system icon that is a filled-in trash can. Now that it's possible to create a body, a button, and some text labels, it's time to consider images.

Creating an Image

An image view is a type of view that is used to display images. In SwiftUI, you typically add an `Image` inside a view's `body` (either in `ContentView` or in a new SwiftUI view file you create). The following code shows an example of a simple image view:

swift

```
struct ImageView: View {
    var body: some View {
        Image("imageName")
            .resizable()
            .scaledToFit()
    }
}
```

This code creates an image view that displays the image asset named imageName. The `resizable()` modifier makes the image view resizable, and the `scaledToFit()` modifier makes the image view fit its container. To run your image view, click the Play button in the top left corner of Xcode. The image view will be displayed in the simulator. Also consider additional modifiers, such as `cornerRadius()` to round the corners of the image view and the `shadow()` modifier to add a shadow to the image view.

User Input Forms

A form view is a type of view that is used to collect user input. In SwiftUI, you build forms with the `Form { ... }` container, which can contain other views, such as text fields, buttons, and labels. The following code shows an example of a simple form view:

swift

```
struct FormView: View {
    @State private var firstName = ""
    @State private var lastName = ""
    @State private var emailAddress = ""
    var body: some View {
        Form {
            Section(header: Text("Name")) {
                TextField("First Name", text: $firstName)
                TextField("Last Name", text: $lastName)
            }
```

```
            Section(header: Text("Email")) {
                TextField("Email Address", text: $emailAddress)
            }
        }
    }
}
```

This code creates a form view that contains two sections. The first section contains two text fields for the user's first and last name. The second section contains a text field for the user's email address. Change the Preview section from our earlier examples to show `FormView` rather than Content `View` to be able to see the changes in the preview screen (Figure 1-5).

***Figure 1-5.** Adding a* `Form`

The `@State` property wrappers are used to store the values of the user's input. The `Form` view uses these values to update the text fields when the user changes them. To run the form view, click the Play button in the top left corner of Xcode. Now it's not just a preview, but an app!

Conclusion

This chapter has been about buttons, forms, images, and other elements that get rendered on a screen. Those can be simplistic at first - but can be used to develop complex and responsive experiences. There are a lot of other options, but these should be enough to get started.

This chapter was not meant to make a reader an expert in user experience. Turns out most systems administrators probably don't need or want to be interface gurus. But we do tend to be able to build experiences just good enough for our needs. Readers that need more should look into books on user interface, user experience, and, of course, SwiftUI.

CHAPTER 2

Variables, Constants, and Data Types

One of the most important aspects of building software is to put information in a spot so it can be recalled. One way is to use a database, but for the purposes of this chapter, we'll cover three primary ways to store data: variables, constants, and data types. To oversimplify what these are:

- Variables are used to store data that can change. The value of a variable can be changed at any time during the execution of a program. Use a variable when the value of the data may change. For example, use a variable to store the current score in a game.
- Constants are used to store data that cannot change. The value of a constant cannot be changed after it is declared. Use a constant when the value of the data will never change. For example, use a constant to store the number of seconds in a minute.
- Data types are used to specify the type of data that a variable or constant can store. Swift has several data types, including integers, floats, strings, and booleans. Use a data type to specify the type of data that a variable or constant can store. This helps to prevent errors and makes your code more readable.

The decision of when to use a variable, constant, or data type depends on the specific needs of your program. Use constants whenever possible. This will make code more reliable and easier to maintain. Also use descriptive names for variables and constants. This will make code easier to understand.

C. Edge et al., *Mastering Swift*, https://doi.org/10.1007/979-8-8688-2770-9_2

Use data types to specify the type of data that your variables and constants can store. This will help to prevent errors and make your code more readable. It's also great to put comments in code anywhere that someone else can't just look at it and intuit what a line or stanza is doing.

Commenting Code

Comments are a great way to explain code to other people, including yourself at a later date. There are two types of comments: single-line comments and multi-line comments. Single-line comments start with two forward slashes (//). Everything after the two forward slashes is ignored by the compiler. For example:

swift

```
// This is a single-line comment.
```

Multi-line comments start with /* and end with */. Everything between them is ignored by the compiler. (Note: /** `...` */ and /// `...` are commonly used for *documentation comments.*) For example:

swift

```
/*
This is a multi-line comment.
It can be used to explain code in more detail.
*/
```

Writing good comments can be tricky. Include enough, but not too much that it's hard to follow. Be clear and concise when writing comments. Explain what the code does, but don't be too long-winded or too detailed. Also use meaningful names for variables, functions, and classes so they are self-explanatory. This will help write shorter and more concise comments. Consistently format the comments and remember to update comments when the code itself changes. Here are some examples of good comments:

swift

```
// This function calculates the factorial of a number.
func factorial(number: Int) -> Int {
  // If the number is 0, return 1.
```

```
  if number == 0 {
    return 1
  } else {
    // Otherwise, recursively calculate the factorial of the number - 1.
    return number * factorial(number: number - 1)
  }
}
// This variable stores the user's name.
var name = ""
// This function displays a welcome message to the user.
func welcome() {
  // Print the user's name.
  print("Welcome, \(name)!")
}
```

Good documentation begins with comments. Both can require discipline to stay on top of. The comments can show others what the code is doing, and to remind yourself, and when used properly can also make code more readable.

Semicolons

Another aspect of Swift that can help with readability is semicolons. Many languages use semicolons to terminate statements and expressions. A statement is a complete unit of code that performs an action. For example, the following code is a statement:

swift

```
print("Hello, world!")
```

This statement prints the string "Hello, world!" to the console. A second statement could then be made on the same line by separating the two with a semicolon:

swift

```
print("Hello, world!"); print("Goodbye, world!")
```

Some languages require a semicolon. They are optional in Swift, unless there are two statements on one line. Some may find it more readable to end a line with them, though. An expression is a combination of values, operators, and functions that evaluates to a single value. For example, the following expression evaluates to the number 12:

swift

```
10 + 2
```

Some may find it more readable to separate statements with semicolons:

swift

```
let answer = 10 + 2;
print("The answer is \(answer)")
```

It's more common to have two statements on a single line in smaller scripts than it is in larger programs. A semicolon can help make a little bit of code easier to troubleshoot, though – even if the compiler doesn't do anything different than it would without them. The reason is how it looks though, and not technical. Now that we've covered a few basics, let's look at how to declare a variable (and all the ways it can be done).

Declare and Use Variables

Variables allow developers to store and manipulate data. Declaring and using variables is straightforward and intuitive. In Swift, variables are declared using the `var` keyword, followed by the chosen variable name. Here's an example where we create a threat score that starts at 100. We can just declare the variable as follows:

swift

```
var score: Int
```

In the above code, we declare a variable named `score` of type `Int`. The type annotation (`: Int`) explicitly specifies the variable's data type as an integer. Once declared, variables can be assigned an initial value using the assignment operator (=). Here's an example:

swift

```
var score: Int = 100
```

In this case, we declare and initialize the `score` variable with an initial value of `100`. Swift allows type inference, so you can omit the type annotation if the initial value is provided:

swift

```
var score = 100
```

Swift automatically infers data types based on assigned value, inferring `Int` in this case. Variables can be accessed and modified throughout your code. Here's an example demonstrating how to use and modify the `score` variable:

swift

```
var score = 100
print("Current score:", score) // Output: Current score: 100
score += 50
print("Updated score:", score) // Output: Updated score: 150
```

The above code first prints the current value of the `score` variable. Then, the value is incremented by 50 using the compound assignment operator (+=). Finally, we print the updated value of the `score` variable. When naming variables, make sure to use descriptive and meaningful names that indicate the variable's purpose. Also start variable names with a lowercase letter and use camel case, such as `userName`, `totalScore`, or `userEmail`. Finally, avoid using reserved keywords or existing function and type names to prevent conflicts. Reserved keywords are typically those that actually do something in a language.

Scope

Scope refers to the part of code where a variable, constant, or other named item is accessible. Items declared at a higher scope are visible to items declared at lower scopes.

There are four main types of scope:

- **Global scope**: Variables and constants declared at global scope are accessible from anywhere in your program.
- **Local scope**: Variables and constants declared inside a function, method, or closure are only accessible within that function, method, or closure.
- **File scope**: In Swift, you can restrict a declaration to a single file using `fileprivate` (or `private` at top level). Without that, a top-level declaration is usually visible to the whole module by default.
- **Nested scope**: Declarations inside a nested block (like an `if`, `for`, `switch`, or a closure) are only visible inside that block.

The following defines a name variable with a global scope, which is then made available to all functions:

swift

```
var name = "Charles"
func greet() {
    // Local scope
    let message = "Hello, \(name)!"
    print(message)
}
greet()
```

The next example shows a variable declared inside the function `greet()`, so it is only accessible within that function:

swift

```
func greet() {
    var name = "Charles"
    // Local scope
    let message = "Hello, \(name)!"
    print(message)
}
greet()
```

The output is the same for each, but if run in the REPL, notice that the following will be shown for the globally declared variable but not for the one defined inside the `greet()` function:

```
name: String = "Charles"
```

This is because once the function returns, local variables go out of scope (and in the REPL, they won't remain bound as top-level names). The next example declares `name` as a property of the `Person` type, and so it can be accessed anywhere `Person` is in scope (and from within the `introduce()` method):

swift

```
struct Person {
    // Type scope (a stored property on the type)
    let name: String
```

```
    func introduce() {
        // Local scope
        let greeting = "Hello, my name is \(name)."
        print(greeting)
    }
}
let charles = Person(name: "Charles")
charles.introduce()
```

In this example, the variable name is declared as a property. Thus, the contents of the struct are available after run including `Person` and any variables included in that struct.

Expressions

Now that there are variables and it's clear when each is available, let's manipulate the data stored in the variable. The most common way to do this, post-declaration, is with an expression. Expressions are used to assign or edit values. Expressions are used to perform calculations, to manipulate data, and to control the flow of your code. Some of the most common expressions in Swift include arithmetic, comparison, logical, and ternary.

The simplest can be arithmetic expressions, which are used to perform mathematical operations. For example, to add numbers and have the result be stored in a variable x, the following uses a let keyword followed by the variable name, followed by an equal sign (=) and then two numbers with a mathematical symbol between them (in this case, a + for addition):

swift

```
let x = 10 + 20
```

Comparison expressions are used to compare values. For example:

swift

```
let x = 10
let y = 20
if x > y {
  print("x is greater than y.")
```

```
} else {
  print("y is greater than x.")
}
```

Logical expressions are used to combine boolean values. For example:

swift

```
let x = true
let y = false
if x && y {
  print("Both x and y are true.")
} else {
  print("Either x or y is false, or both are false.")
}
```

Ternary expressions are used to evaluate a boolean expression and return one of two values depending on the result. For example:

swift

```
let x = 10
let y = 20
let largerNumber = x > y ? x : y
```

The above results in the following when run from the REPL:

swift

```
x: Int = 10
y: Int = 20
largerNumber: Int = 20
```

The variables used thus far have just been defined, but one aspect that can be frustrating is isolating what variables are available in different parts of code.

Global and Local Variables

Global variables are declared outside of any function or class, while local variables are declared inside of a function or class. Use global variables sparingly and only when necessary.

Use local variables for data that is specific to the function or class in which it is used.

When using global variables, document your code clearly so that other programmers can understand how the variables are used.

Global variables have a global scope, meaning that they can be accessed from anywhere in the program. This can be useful for storing data that needs to be shared by multiple functions or classes. However, it is important to use global variables sparingly, as they can make your code more difficult to read and maintain.

Local variables have a local scope, meaning that they can only be accessed from within the function or class in which they are declared. This is the preferred way to declare variables, as it helps to encapsulate your code and makes it more reusable.

Here are some examples of global and local variables in Swift:

swift

```
// Global variable
let currentYear = 2023
// Local variable
func multiply(a: Int, b: Int) -> Int {
  let product = a * b
  return product
}
// Global variable can be accessed from anywhere in the program
print(currentYear) // Outputs 2023
// Local variable can only be accessed from within the multiply() function
let result = multiply(a: 2, b: 3)
print(result) // Outputs 6
```

Top-level globals (and `static` stored properties) with initial values are lazily initialized: their initializer runs once, the first time the value is accessed. Local variables, on the other hand, are evaluated immediately when execution reaches their declaration. Both kinds of values can be declared with the `let` or `var` keyword.

Inferring Type

Type inference allows the compiler to infer the type of a variable or expression based on its value. This can make code more concise and easier to read. For example, the following declares a variable called x and assigns it the value 10. The compiler can infer that the type of x is `Int` because the value 10 is an integer.

swift

```
var x = 10
```

Type inference can also be used with expressions. For example, the following code calculates 5 times 4. The compiler can infer that the type of the expression is `Int` because the product of two integers is an integer.

swift

```
let product = 5 * 4
```

Lazy evaluation is a general idea (deferring work until it's needed). In Swift specifically, the `lazy` keyword applies to *stored properties* on a type, not to local variables. A `lazy` stored property's initializer runs the first time that property is accessed. For example:

swift

```
final class Example {
  lazy var x = 5 * 4
}
let example = Example()
print(example.x) // First access initializes x
```

Swift is a statically typed language. Static typing is where the data type of a variable is known at compile time. This means that the compiler can check for errors in the code before it is executed. Static typing is often seen as being more reliable than dynamic typing, as it can help to prevent errors from occurring. This isn't to say that type has to be explicit in the code, but at compile time, it is rendered as explicit. Thus, it can seem as though Swift is a dynamically typed language.

Dynamic typing is a form of typing where the data type of a variable is not known at compile time. This means that the compiler cannot check for errors in the code before it is executed. Dynamic typing is often seen as being more flexible than static typing, as it allows the data type of a variable to change during the execution of the code. Dynamic typing is also considered less secure as the type checks can't be done until the user is actually running the code.

With type inference and other features of Swift, the developer gets the best of both worlds; however, given that the type will be known at compile time, it's still best to be explicit about typing when possible.

Number Literals

Number literals are constants that represent numbers. They are used to represent values such as integers and floating-point numbers. There are two main types of number literals in Swift: integer literals and floating-point literals.

Integer literals represent whole numbers. They can be written in decimal, octal, binary, or hexadecimal form, as follows:

swift

```
10   // Decimal
0o10 // Octal
0b01 // Binary
0xA  // Hexadecimal
```

Floating-point literals represent real numbers. They can be written in decimal or scientific notation, as follows:

swift

```
1.23   // Decimal
1.23e4 // Scientific notation
```

Boolean literals represent the values true and false, as seen below:

swift

```
true
false
```

Number literals can be used in a variety of ways in Swift code. They can be used to initialize variables, to perform mathematical operations, and to compare values.

Here are some examples of how number literals can be used in Swift code:

swift

```
var myInteger = 10
var myFirstFloatingPoint = 5.0
var mySecondFloatingPoint = 1.23
print(myFirstFloatingPoint + mySecondFloatingPoint) // Prints 6.23
if myInteger == 10 {
  print("The value of myInteger is 10")
}
```

It's usually best to use the type that represents your data accurately and clearly. Storage sizes vary (e.g., on 64-bit platforms, `Int` and `Double` are commonly 8 bytes, while `Bool` is typically at least a byte), and strings are variable-sized based on their contents. Some things to consider when using number literals to represent numbers:

- Use underscores to make your code more readable. For example, you could write the number literal 1_000_000 instead of 1000000.
- Use scientific notation for large or small numbers. For example, you could write the number literal 1.23e4 instead of 12300.
- Use boolean literals to represent the values true and false.

The type of a variable is fixed at compile time in Swift, but you can convert values between types when you need to.

Number Type Conversion

Convert between different number types by wrapping existing number values in parentheses preceded by the type of the desired result. For example:

swift

```
let anInteger = 10
let aFloatingPoint = Double(anInteger)
let backToAnInteger = Int(aFloatingPoint)
```

In this example, we first assigned the number 10 to a new variable, which caused the type of that variable to be inferred as `Int`. Then, we converted our integer to the floating point value 10.0 by wrapping it in parentheses preceded by the desired result type `Double`.

We can use a similar approach to convert strings to numbers. For example:

swift

```
let stringNumber = "10"
let intNumber = Int(stringNumber)!
let doubleNumber = Double(stringNumber)!
```

In this example, first we create a variable called `stringNumber` which contains the string "10". We then convert our string to both a `Double` and an `Int` using the method from the previous example. One difference to notice however is that we have added exclamation points after the conversions. As discussed in the chapter on optionals, this is because the result of attempting to convert a String to an Int is actually not an Int, but rather an *optional* Int, which is written as Int?. An Int? (optional integer) may contain an integer, or it may contain "nothing" (a.k.a. "nil"), and this is where the term "optional" arises from. The exclamation point is effectively a second step of the conversion, which allows us to convert from Int? to Int. It can be understood in this context to mean "Check if this optional integer contains an actual integer (as opposed to "nil"), and if it does, then return that integer as a (non-optional) Int. If it contains "nil" instead of an integer, then simply crash."

Integer Bounds

Integer bounds define the minimum and maximum values that an integer type can represent. This information is used by the compiler to ensure that integer values are used safely and correctly. There are two types of integer bounds: signed and unsigned. Signed bounds define the minimum and maximum values that a signed integer type can represent. Signed integers can represent both positive and negative values. Unsigned bounds define the minimum and maximum values that an unsigned integer type can represent. Unsigned integers can only represent positive values.

The integer bounds for each type in Swift are defined in Table 2-1.

Table 2-1. *Types and Bounds of Integers in Swift*

Type	Signed Bounds	Unsigned Bounds
Int8	-128 to 127	0 to 255
Int16	-32768 to 32767	0 to 65535
Int32	-2147483648 to 2147483647	0 to 4294967295
Int64	-9223372036854775808 to 9223372036854775807	0 to 18446744073709551615
UInt8	0 to 255	
UInt16	0 to 65535	
UInt32	0 to 4294967295	
UInt64	0 to 18446744073709551615	

Integer bounds can be used to validate the values of integer variables, ensure that integer values are used within their valid ranges, and calculate the size of integer data structures. Here is an example of how integer bounds can be used to validate the values of integer variables:

swift

```
let minValue = Int16(Int8.min)
let maxValue = Int16(Int8.max)
let number: Int16 = 128
if number < minValue || number > maxValue {
  print("The value of number is out of bounds.")
} else {
  print("The value of number is within bounds.")
}
```

In the above example, the `minValue` and `maxValue` constants are used to represent the minimum and maximum values that an `Int8` variable can represent. The number variable is then initialized with a value of 128, which is outside of the valid range for an `Int8` variable. The if statement then checks to see if the value of number is out of bounds. If it is, the first `print()` statement will be executed. Otherwise, the second `print()` statement will be executed.

The reason we specified the type of `number` as being `Int16` is because a compilation error would result if you tried to store the integer literal `128` into a variable of type `Int8` (since `Int8.max` is `127`).

This type of linting allows for more advanced troubleshooting and unit testing, as the needs of code within a project evolve.

Raw Values

An enumeration case is a value that is a member of an enumeration. Enumerations are a way to define a set of related values. For example, you could create an enumeration for the days of the week, the states of a traffic light, or the different types of coins. Raw values are a way to assign unique values to enumeration cases. They can be of any basic data type, such as integers, strings, or characters. To use raw values in an enumeration, specify the raw-value type when an enumeration is declared. To declare an enumeration case, use the case keyword. For example, the following code declares an enumeration for tasks an admin might perform on a device, defined as integers:

swift

```
enum AdminTask: Int {
  case makeAdmin = 1
  case removeAdmin = 2
  case clearCache = 3
  case addToken = 4
}
```

In this example, the raw-value type for AdminTask is Int. This means that each case in the enumeration is assigned an integer value. The makeAdmin case is assigned the value 1, the removeAdmin case is assigned the value 2, and so on. Use the raw value of an enumeration case to compare two cases or to convert an enumeration case to a different data type. For example:

swift

```
let task = AdminTask.makeAdmin
if task == .makeAdmin {
  print("The user will be made an admin.")
}
let taskNumber = task.rawValue
print(taskNumber) // 1
```

In this example, the variable called task is defined and set equal to the .makeAdmin case in the AdminTask enumeration. Then, the if statement checks if the task is equal to the .makeAdmin case. If the result is true, the code inside the if statement will be executed. In this case, the code inside the if statement will print the message "The user will be made an admin."

Next, the rawValue of the task is retrieved. In this case, the raw value is 1. We then print the retrieved raw value to the console.

Raw values are useful because it is sometimes helpful to associate a corresponding value of a different type to each case of an enumeration. For example, if the raw value is of type Int, you may find a use case for retrieving the raw value of a case, adding 1 to it, and then creating a value of the enumeration type using that incremented raw value. An enumeration with raw values will have an initializer which takes an argument called rawValue and which returns the case that corresponds to the given raw value, or nil if the given raw value does not correspond to any case. For example:

swift

```
let makeAdminTask = AdminTask.makeAdmin
let incrementedRawValue = makeAdminTask.rawValue + 1
let removeAdminTask = AdminTask(rawValue: incrementedRawValue)!
print(removeAdminTask) // .removeAdmin
```

If the raw value type is `Int`, then most of the values can be implicitly assigned to the cases, like this:

swift

```
enum AdminTask: Int {
    case makeAdmin = 1
    case removeAdmin
    case clearCache
    case addToken
}
```

The subsequent cases will automatically take on the integer values that follow the initial integer value that is explicitly provided. This can make it a little more convenient to declare the enumeration. However, it is important to note that the raw values are assigned automatically, so you cannot control them. This means that if you add or remove enumeration cases, the raw values for the other enumeration cases may change.

The tasks are a finite, simple example of enumerations, but there are much more intricate uses, such as recursive enumerations.

Recursive Enumerations

A recursive enumeration is a special type of enumeration in which one or more cases have another instance of the enumeration as one of their associated values. This allows data to be represented in a nested structure.

To create a recursive enumeration, you use the indirect keyword either before the enumeration declaration or before the recursive case. This tells the compiler that the cases (or just the explicitly marked cases) can refer to the enumeration. Here is an example of a recursive enumeration to represent a linked list:

swift

```
indirect enum LinkedList {
```

```
  case empty
  case node(value: Int, next: LinkedList)
}
```

This enumeration has two cases: empty and node. The node case has an associated value of (value: `Int`, next: `LinkedList`). The next associated value is also a `LinkedList`, which means that the `LinkedList` enumeration can represent a linked list of any length. Here is an example of how to use the `LinkedList` enumeration:

swift

```
let list: LinkedList = .node(value: 1, next: .node(value: 2, next:
.node(value: 3, next: .empty)))
// Print the contents of the linked list
func printList(_ list: LinkedList) {
    switch list {
    case .empty:
        break
    case .node(let value, let next):
        print(value)
        printList(next)
    }
}
printList(list)
```

This code will print the following output:

swift

```
1
2
3
```

Recursive enumerations can be used to represent a variety of data structures, such as trees, graphs, and binary trees.

Mutability

Variables can be either mutable (changeable) or immutable (constant). Mutable variables are declared using the var keyword, while immutable variables are declared using the let keyword. It is generally recommended to use immutable variables (so defined with a let statement) whenever the value does not need to be modified, as it enhances code clarity and safety. For example, if a user on a machine was identified with a userName variable and that user has a maximum defer time of 14 days for software updates, defined as maxDefer that we don't want to be able to change, that could be represented as the following:

swift

```
var userName = "John"
let maxDefer = 14
userName = "Mike" // Mutable variable
// maxDefer = 200 // Error: Cannot assign to 'let' value 'maxDefer'
```

In the example above, userName is a mutable variable that can be modified, whereas maxDefer is an immutable variable that cannot be reassigned after its initial value is set. This allows for different users to be able to use the system but for the maximum deferral to not be changed, despite other things that might happen in code.

Understanding Data Types

Data types define the kind of data that can be stored and manipulated. The most common are booleans, integers, and strings. Strings represent a sequence of characters, such as words, sentences, or symbols. Strings are declared using the String data type. Here's an example of a message that can be displayed to a user to get them to reboot a computer:

swift

```
let message: String = "Please Restart The Computer"
print(message)
```

In the above code, we declare a constant named message of type String and assign it the value "Please Restart The Computer". Strings can be concatenated using the + operator or interpolated using the \() syntax.

swift

```
let strings = ["Please", "Restart", "The", "Computer"]
let message = strings.joined(separator: " ")
print(message)
```

The result from the above code is the same as the first example. This isn't used with other types, such as with integers.

Integers

Integers represent whole numbers without decimal places. In Swift, there are different types of integers available, such as `Int`, `Int8`, `Int16`, `Int32`, and `Int64`, each representing different ranges of values. The `Int` type is commonly used and automatically selected by Swift in most cases. Here's an example:

swift

```
let age: Int = 25
```

In the above code, we declare a constant named `age` of type `Int` and assign it the value `25`. Integers can be used for arithmetic operations, comparisons, and other numerical computations.

Floating-Point Numbers

Floating-point numbers represent decimal numbers. In Swift, there are two types of floating-point numbers: `Float` and `Double`. The `Double` type provides higher precision than `Float` and is the default choice for floating-point numbers. Here's an example:

swift

```
let pi: Double = 3.14159
```

In the above code, we declare a constant named `pi` of type `Double` and assign it the value `3.14159`. Floating-point numbers can be used for mathematical calculations involving decimal values.

Boolean Values

Boolean values represent either true or false. In Swift, the `Bool` type is used to represent boolean values. Here's an example:

swift

```
let isRaining: Bool = true
```

In the above code, we declare a constant named `isRaining` of type `Bool` and assign it the value `true`. Boolean values are often used in conditional statements, comparisons, and decision-making processes.

Type Inference

Thel type inference system in Swift means that developers don't always have to explicitly declare the data type of a variable. Swift can automatically infer the type based on the initial value assigned. Here's an example where `userName` will be a string and `threatScore` becomes a double (with comments inline):

swift

```
let userName = "Charles" // Swift infers the type as String
let threatScore = 25.5 // Swift infers the type as Double
```

In the above code, we omit the explicit type declarations, and Swift infers the data types based on the assigned values. To extend the example, we can then build multiple tasks in a sequence by passing the output of one string to another and then another. In the following example, we can take a long `userName` and remove the spaces to get a short name:

swift

```
let userName = "Charles Edge"
let words = userName.split(separator: " ")
let concatenatedString = words.joined()
print(concatenatedString)
```

The above code simply concatenates the string or joins it without the separator.

Type Identifiers

Type identifiers are strings that are used to uniquely identify types in Swift. Types identifier should give a clear indication of the type that it represents. For example, the type identifier MyModel clearly indicates that the type is a model. If using multiple types in code, try to use consistent type identifiers for similar types. Generic type identifiers can be useful, but they can also make code more difficult to follow.

Type identifiers can be used to declare variables and constants of a specific type. For example, the following code declares a variable of type `String` and assigns it the value "iOS":

swift

```
let operatingSystem = "iOS"
```

Type identifiers can refer to types in function parameters and return values. For example, the following code defines a function that takes a `String` as its input and returns a `Double`:

swift

```
func calculateLength(of string: String) -> Double {
  return string.count
}
```

The above -> operator is used to specify the return type of a function or closure.

Type identifiers are case-sensitive and must be unique within a given scope. They can be any string of characters, but they are typically composed of alphanumeric characters, underscores, and periods. Here are some examples of valid type identifiers:

- `MyType`
- `MyModel`
- `MyAPI`
- `MyType.MyNestedType`
- `Vector3`
- `StateMachine_tests`

- Here are some examples of invalid type identifiers:
  - `my-type` (hyphens are not allowed)
  - `My Type` (spaces are not allowed)
  - `.MyType` (type identifiers never start with a period)

A property is a variable or constant that is associated with a type. Type properties are another aspect of types that will be used frequently.

Type Properties

Type properties are properties that are associated with a type, rather than with an instance of a type. This means that all instances of a type share the same value for a type property. Here are some examples of how type properties can be used:

- **Storing shared data**: A type property can be used to store shared data that is used by all instances of a type. For example, a type property could be used to store the current user, the current date, or the current time.
- **Implementing constants**: A type property can be used to implement a constant that is associated with a type. For example, a type property could be used to implement the constant π.
- **Providing default values for properties**: A type property can be used to provide a default value for a property. For example, a type property could be used to provide a default value for the name property of a struct.

Type properties are declared using the static keyword. For example, the following code declares a type property called pi of type `Double`:

swift

```
static let pi = 3.14159
```

Type properties can be accessed using the type name, followed by a dot, followed by the name of the type property. For example, the following code prints the value of the pi type property:

swift

```
print(MyType.pi)
```

Type properties can be of any type, including structs, classes, enumerations, and even other type properties. There are two types of type properties: stored type properties and computed type properties. Stored type properties are properties that have a constant or variable value that is stored with the type. For example, the pi type property is a stored type property. Computed type properties are properties that do not have a stored value. Instead, the value of a computed type property is computed each time it is accessed. For example, the following code declares a computed type property called computerType that returns a string with a computer type:

swift

```
static var greeting: String {
  return "macOS"
}
```

Type properties can be used to store shared data, implement constants, and provide default values for properties. This can become a lot to manage, and many overlap - which is one reason to use type aliases.

Type Aliases

A type alias is a way to give a new name to an existing type. By giving a more meaningful name to an existing type, you can make your code easier to read and understand for other developers. Type aliases also help to make code more concise. Sometimes, it can be more concise to use a type alias instead of the full name of the type. For example, a type alias called `Coordinate` could be used for the `(Double, Double)` type. This would allow a statement like let coordinate: `Coordinate` = (3.14, 1.57) instead of let coordinate: `(Double, Double)` = (3.14, 1.57).

To create a type alias, use the typealias keyword. The syntax for creating a type alias is as follows:

swift

```
typealias <new_name> = <existing_type>
```

For example, the following code creates a type alias called `Coordinate` for the `(Double, Double)` type:

swift

```
typealias Coordinate = (Double, Double)
```

Once created, a type alias is used just like any other type. For example, the following code creates a variable of type `Coordinate` and assigns it the value (3.14, 1.57):

swift

```
var coordinate: Coordinate = (3.14, 1.57)
```

Chaining types with type aliases makes it simpler to define multiple similar types at once.

Type Inference and Explicit Type Declarations

Type inference and explicit type declarations are key concepts that govern how data types are handled. Type inference allows Swift to automatically deduce the data type of a variable based on its assigned value, while explicit type declarations provide developers with control over explicitly specifying the data type. In the next few sections, we will explore both type inference and explicit type declarations.

Type Inference

Type inference enables the compiler to automatically deduce the data type of a variable based on its assigned value. This means you don't always have to explicitly declare the data type of a variable. Here's an example:

swift

```
let name = "John"
```

In the above code, the compiler infers that the `name` variable is of type `String` based on the assigned value, which is a string literal. Type inference makes code more concise and eliminates the need for redundant type annotations, especially when the type can be easily determined from the context.

Explicit Type Declarations

While type inference is powerful, there are situations where explicit type declarations are beneficial, for example, if the intended type isn't immediately apparent from the assigned value or if the variable needs to be of a specific type, regardless of the assigned value.

Explicitly declaring the data type of a variable provides clarity and makes the code more self-documenting. It also helps catch potential type-related errors during development. Here's an example of an explicit type declaration:

swift

```
let age: Double = 25
```

In the above code, we explicitly declare the age variable as a Double (floating point), which overpowers the inference of Int that would have occurred otherwise.

Choosing Between Type Inference and Explicit Type Declarations

The choice between type inference and explicit type declarations depends on the specific circumstances and coding style preferences. Consider the following guidelines:

- Use type inference when the type can be easily determined from the assigned value or when the context makes the type apparent.
- Employ explicit type declarations when clarity and self-documentation are crucial or when you want to ensure a specific type regardless of the assigned value.

To help us not make mistakes, Xcode often points us in directions when we're not practicing type safety where needed. For example, the error shown in Figure 2-1 indicates that the compiler is going to use CFString but also acknowledges that this might not be desired.

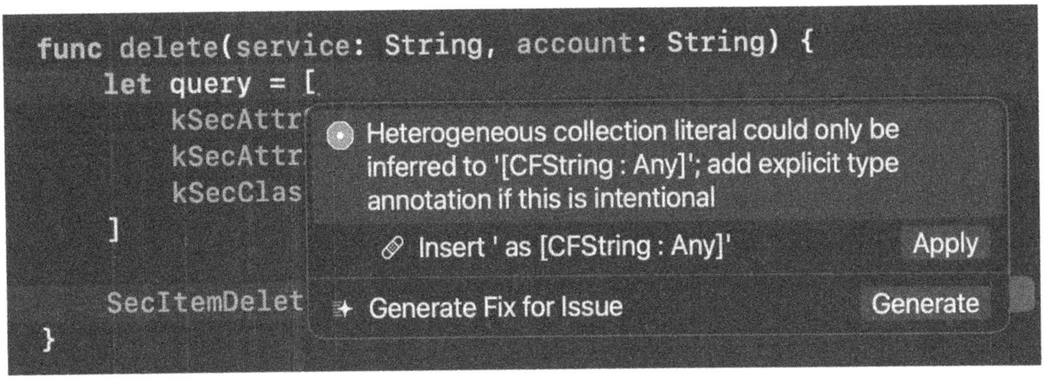

Figure 2-1. *Xcode Error with Suggested Fixes*

A heterogeneous collection literal is a collection literal that can contain elements of different types. For example, the following is a heterogeneous collection literal that contains a string, an integer, and a boolean:

swift

```
[ "hello", 10, true ]
```

Heterogeneous collection literals were introduced in Swift 3.0. Before Swift 3.0, collection literals could only contain elements of the same type. When you create a heterogeneous collection literal, Swift will infer the type of the collection to be Any. This means that you can store any type of element in the collection, but you will need to cast the elements to their appropriate types when you access them.

For example, the following code will print the string "hello" and the integer 10:

swift

```
let heterogeneousCollection = [ "hello", 10, true ]
print(heterogeneousCollection[0] as! String)
print(heterogeneousCollection[1] as! Int)
```

In Swift 5.8, a new warning was introduced for heterogeneous collection literals. This warning is triggered when a heterogeneous collection literal is inferred to be of type Any. The warning suggests that you should explicitly specify the type of the collection to avoid type safety issues. You can silence the warning indicated earlier by explicitly specifying the type of the collection.

Type Annotations for Functions and Complex Types

In addition to variables, type inference and explicit type declarations also apply to functions and complex types. When defining function parameters or return types, explicit type annotations can provide clarity and improve code readability. Similarly, explicit type declarations are beneficial when dealing with complex types, such as dictionaries or arrays, where the contained data type may not be immediately obvious.

Understanding type inference and explicit type declarations in Swift is crucial for writing clean, maintainable, and expressive code. Type inference allows the compiler to deduce the data type automatically, reducing verbosity and enhancing code conciseness. On the other hand, explicit type declarations provide clarity, self-documentation, and catch potential type-related errors during development. By using a combination of type inference and explicit type declarations strategically, you can strike a balance between code readability, conciseness, and clarity in your Swift.

Type Extensions

Extensions add new functionality to an existing type. Extensions can add new methods, computed properties, and initializers to a type. They can also override existing methods and properties. To create an extension, use the extension keyword. For example, the following code creates an extension for the `String` type that adds a new method called `trimmed()`:

swift

```
extension String {
    func trimmed() -> String {
        return self.trimmingCharacters(in: .whitespacesAndNewlines)
    }
}
```

The `trimmed()` method takes no arguments and returns a new `String` instance that has been trimmed of whitespace and newline characters. Extensions can be used to add new functionality to any type, including classes, structures, and enumerations. They can also be used to add new functionality to protocols.

More on Types

A type defines what type of data can be stored in a given variable. Mastery of types is a constantly evolving skill, as it has been for 40+ years.

Associated Types

Associated types are used to define protocols that can be used with different types. This can be useful to make code more reusable. Associated types can define a protocol that is used with different types, without having to duplicate code. They're also used to encapsulate type information in a protocol, which can make code more readable and maintainable. Associated types are also useful to provide generic APIs that can be used with different types.

To define an associated type, use the associatedtype keyword. The syntax for defining an associated type is as follows:

swift

```
protocol MyProtocol {
  associatedtype DataType
}
```

The `DataType` associated type is a placeholder for the type that will be used with the `MyProtocol` protocol. The `DataType` associated type can be any type, including structs, classes, enumerations, and even other protocols.

Once you have defined an associated type, you can use it in the protocol's methods and properties. For example, the following protocol defines an associated type called `DataType` and a method called `add(_:)` that takes a `DataType` as its input:

swift

```
protocol MyProtocol {
  associatedtype DataType
  func add(_ value: DataType)
}
```

A conforming type must provide an implementation for the `add(_:)` method that takes a `DataType` as its input. The conforming type must also specify the type that will be used for the `DataType` associated type.

Here is an example of a conforming type that uses the `MyProtocol` protocol:

swift

```
struct MyType: MyProtocol {
  typealias DataType = Int
  func add(_ value: Int) {
      print(value)
  }
}
```

The `MyType` struct conforms to the `MyProtocol` protocol by providing an implementation for the `add(_:)` method that takes an `Int` as its input. The `MyType` struct also specifies that the `DataType` associated type will be of type `Int`.

Generic where clauses with associated types in Swift allow you to specify constraints on the associated types of a protocol. This can be useful when requiring that the associated type conform to a certain protocol: For example, it's possible to require that the associated type conform to the Comparable protocol, which would ensure that the associated type can be compared to other values of the same type. They can also require that the associated type have a certain property or method or require that the associated type be of a certain type, like to require that the associated type be of type Int or String.

To use a generic where clause with associated types, you use the where keyword. The syntax for using a generic where clause with associated types is as follows:

swift

```
protocol MyProtocol {
  associatedtype DataType where
    DataType: Comparable
}
```

The where clause specifies the constraints on the associated type. In this example, the constraint is that the associated type must conform to the Comparable protocol. Once an associated type is declared, you can use it in the protocol's methods and properties. For example, the following protocol defines a method called sort() that takes an array of DataType elements as its input and sorts it:

swift

```
protocol MyProtocol {
  associatedtype DataType where
    DataType: Comparable
  func sort(array: [DataType])
}
```

A conforming type must provide an implementation for the sort() method that takes a DataType as its input. The conforming type must also ensure that the DataType associated type conforms to the Comparable protocol. For example, a conforming type that uses the MyProtocol protocol:

swift

```
struct MyType: MyProtocol {
  typealias DataType = Int
```

```
  func sort(array: [Int]) {
    // Sort the elements of the DataType array
  }
}
```

The `MyType` struct conforms to the `MyProtocol` protocol by providing an implementation for the `sort()` method that takes an array of Ints as its input. The `MyType` struct also ensures that the `DataType` associated type is of type `Int`.

Generic Type Parameters

Generic type parameters in Swift allow you to write generic code that can be used with different types of data. This can make your code more reusable and flexible. A type parameter of a function is declared by writing its name surrounded by angle brackets immediately after the function's name. For example, the following function has a type parameter called T:

swift

```
func swapTwoValues<T>(_ a: inout T, _ b: inout T) {
  var temp = a
  a = b
  b = temp
}
```

This function can be used to swap the values of two variables of any type. For example, use it to swap the values of two integers, two strings, or two arrays. To use the `swapTwoValues()` function, you simply specify the type of the variables that you want to swap when you call the function. For example, the following code swaps the values of two integers:

swift

```
var a = 1
var b = 2
swapTwoValues(&a, &b)
print(a) // Outputs 2
print(b) // Outputs 1
```

Type parameters can also be used to define generic classes and structs. For example, the following class defines a generic stack:

swift

```
class Stack<T> {
  private var elements: [T] = []
  func push(_ element: T) {
    elements.append(element)
  }
  func pop() -> T? {
    return elements.popLast()
  }
  var isEmpty: Bool {
    return elements.isEmpty
  }
}
```

This class can be used to store a stack of data of any type, for example, to store a stack of integers, a stack of strings, or a stack of objects. To use the `Stack` class, specify the type of data to store in the stack when creating a new instance of the class. For example, the following code creates a stack of integers:

swift

```
let stack = Stack<Int>()
stack.push(1)
stack.push(2)
stack.push(3)
let poppedElement = stack.pop()
print(poppedElement) // Outputs 3
```

The return would appear as follows:

swift

```
Optional(3)
stack: Stack<Int> = {
```

```
  elements = 2 values {
    [0] = 1
    [1] = 2
  }
}
poppedElement: Int? = 3
```

In addition to type parameters, which are used to structure data, it's also good to understand other type concepts, like generic types.

Type Constraints

Type constraints are used to constrain the types that can be used for a given type parameter. This can be useful for writing generic code that can work with different types of data, or for enforcing specific requirements on the types that can be used with a given function or type. Constraints can be applied to type parameters by writing a colon after the name of the type parameter and then writing an ampersand (&) separated list of the protocols which constrain the parameter. Constraints can be applied to the associated types of type parameters by using the where keyword followed by a list of constraints. For example, the following function has a type parameter T with a type constraint that requires T to conform to the `Equatable` protocol:

swift

```
func swapTwoValues<T: Equatable>(_ a: inout T, _ b: inout T) {
  var temp = a
  a = b
  b = temp
}
```

This function can only be used to swap the values of two variables of a type that conforms to the `Equatable` protocol, such as integers or strings. Type parameters of custom types can be constrained in the same way. For example, the following struct defines a generic `Stack` that can only store values of a type that conforms to the `Equatable` protocol:

swift

```
struct Stack<T: Equatable> {
  private var elements: [T] = []
  func push(_ element: T) {
    elements.append(element)
  }
  func pop() -> T? {
    return elements.popLast()
  }
  var isEmpty: Bool {
    return elements.isEmpty
  }
}
```

This struct can only be used to create a stack of values of a type that conforms to the `Equatable` protocol. Further, constraints can be applied to associated types. Opaque types can also be used to define more opinionated code.

It is also possible to have unnamed type parameters. This is done by using the `some` keyword followed by the names of the constraining protocols. For example:

swift

```
func drawShape(shape: some Shape) {
  shape.draw()
}
// This function can be used to draw any type of shape, without needing to
know the specific type of the shape.
let circle = Circle()
drawShape(shape: circle)
```

One can use type parameters to improve abstraction:

swift

```
class ViewController: UIViewController {
  private let shape: any Shape
  init(shape: some Shape) {
    self.shape = shape
  }
```

```
  override func viewDidLoad() {
    super.viewDidLoad()
    // Draw the shape on the view.
    shape.draw()
  }
}
// This view controller can be used to display any type of shape, without
needing to know the specific type of the shape.
let circle = Circle()
let viewController = ViewController(shape: circle)
```

Type parameters can also be used to reduce coupling between different parts of your code:

swift

```
// File 1
protocol Shape {
  func draw()
}
// File 2
class Circle: Shape {
  func draw() {
    // Draw a circle.
  }
}
// File 3
func drawShape(shape: some Shape) {
  shape.draw()
}
// File 4
let circle = Circle()
drawShape(shape: circle)
```

In this example, the drawShape() function does not need to know the specific type of the shape that it is drawing. This is because the drawShape() function is only interested in the capabilities of the shape, not its specific type.

Opaque Result Types

Opaque result types hide the specific type of a value returned from a function, while still exposing its capabilities. This is useful for encapsulating data, improving abstraction, and reducing coupling between different parts of your code.

To use an opaque result type, one uses the `some` keyword followed by the name of a protocol which describes the capabilities that will be exposed. For example, let's consider a protocol named `Shape`:

swift

```
protocol Shape {
  func draw()
}
```

We could use this protocol in an opaque result type like this:

swift

```
func standardButtonShape() -> some Shape {
  return Circle()
}
```

Boxed Protocol Types

Boxed protocol types store an instance of any type that conforms to a given protocol. This can be useful for writing generic code that can work with different types of data or for storing data in a way that is independent of its specific type.

To create a boxed protocol type, use the any keyword followed by the name of the protocol. For example, the following code creates a boxed protocol type for the `CustomStringConvertible` protocol:

swift

```
let boxedCustomStringConvertible: any CustomStringConvertible = 1
```

This variable can now store any value that conforms to the `CustomStringConvertible` protocol (`Int`, `Bool`, etc.). Boxed protocol types can be used in a variety of ways, for example, to write a generic function that can work with different types of data, as follows:

swift

```
func concatenateDescriptions(_ a: any CustomStringConvertible, _ b: any
CustomStringConvertible) -> String {
  return a.description + b.description
}
// This function can be used to concatenate the descriptions of two values
that conform to the CustomStringConvertible protocol.
let result = concatenateDescriptions(15, true)
print(result) // "15true"
```

Boxed protocol types can also store data in a way that is independent of its specific type:

swift

```
let data: [any Equatable] = [1, "hello", MyEquatableObject()]
```

This array can now store any type of data that conforms to the `Equatable` protocol, regardless of its specific type. The data stored in the type can be changed.

Constants and Their Usage

Constants are variables whose values cannot be changed once assigned. They provide a way to store and refer to fixed values throughout your code. Constants are useful when there are values that are known (and so objects can be substantiated intentionally) and will remain unchanged. This allows the compiler to make optimizations and can potentially improve overall performance.

The following are few examples of good use cases for constants:

- **Mathematical or scientific constants**: Use constants to store fixed values like π (`let pi = 3.14159`), the speed of light, or any other mathematical or scientific constant used in calculations.
- **Configuration values**: Constants can store configuration values that remain the same throughout the execution of your program, such as API endpoints, database connection strings, or application-specific settings.

- **Magic numbers**: Instead of using hard-coded values in your code, assign them to constants with meaningful names. This improves code readability and allows you to make changes in a single place if the value needs to be updated.
- **Enumerations**: Constants are often used in conjunction with enumerations to define a set of related values that remain constant.

Constants are declared using the `let` keyword, followed by the chosen constant name and an assigned value. Here's an example:

swift

```
let maximumAttempts = 3
```

In the above code, a constant named `maximumAttempts` is declared with an assigned value of `3`. Once a constant is assigned a value, it cannot be changed.

Using Constants

Let's see an example of using constants in a practical scenario. The following defines a threat score based on attributes that represent a given desired security posture vs. that gleaned from a computer. There are 30 users and the loop will evaluate the threat scores of some of these, defined in `threatScores`:

swift

```
let numberOfUsers = 30
let passingScore = 70
var threatScores: [Int] = [85, 90, 65, 70, 95, 80]
for score in threatScores {
    if score >= passingScore {
        print("Device is in compliance!")
    } else {
        print("Device is not in compliance!")
    }
}
```

In the above code, `numberOfUsers` and `passingScore` are constants representing the total number of users and the minimum passing score, respectively. These constants are used to evaluate the scores of different users in the loop, making the code more readable and easier to modify.

Assigning Constant Properties During Initialization

Constant properties can have values assigned during initialization. This means the developer can set the value of a constant property once, and it cannot be changed thereafter. To do so, use the let keyword followed by the name of the property and the value to be assigned. For example, the following code shows how to assign a value to a constant property called name during initialization:

swift

```
class Person {
  let name: String
  init(name: String) {
    self.name = name
  }
}
let person = Person(name: "John Doe")
print(person.name) // Outputs "John Doe"
```

The value of the name property cannot be reassigned after it has been initialized. If you try to do so, you will get a compile-time error. This can be used to improve the immutability of code. Its value cannot be changed accidentally or maliciously be changed.

Developers can also assign values to constants during initialization to improve the performance of your code. When the compiler knows that a property is constant, it can optimize the code accordingly. For example, the compiler may be able to inline the code that accesses the property, or it may be able to avoid allocating memory for the property.

Basic Arithmetic Operations and String Manipulation

Performing basic arithmetic operations and manipulating strings are fundamental skills for building applications. This is done using assignment operators. There are two types of assignment operators: simple assignment operators and compound assignment operators. Simple assignment operators assign the value on the right side of the operator to the variable on the left side of the operator. The simple assignment operator is the following:

- =: Assigns the value on the right side of the operator to the variable on the left side of the operator

Compound assignment operators combine an assignment operation with an arithmetic or logical operation. The following are the compound assignment operators in Swift:

- +=: Adds the value on the right side of the operator to the variable on the left side of the operator and assigns the result to the variable on the left side of the operator
- -=: Subtracts the value on the right side of the operator from the variable on the left side of the operator and assigns the result to the variable on the left side of the operator
- *=: Multiplies the value on the right side of the operator by the variable on the left side of the operator and assigns the result to the variable on the left side of the operator
- /=: Divides the value on the left side of the operator by the value on the right side of the operator and assigns the result to the variable on the left side of the operator
- %=: Divides the value on the left side of the operator by the value on the right side of the operator and assigns the remainder to the variable on the left side of the operator
- <<=: Shifts the value on the left side of the operator to the left by the number of bits specified by the value on the right side of the operator and assigns the result to the variable on the left side of the operator

- =: Shifts the value on the left side of the operator to the right by the number of bits specified by the value on the right side of the operator and assigns the result to the variable on the left side of the operator
- &=: Performs a bitwise AND operation on the value on the left side of the operator and the value on the right side of the operator and assigns the result to the variable on the left side of thc operator
- |=: Performs a bitwise OR operation on the value on the left side of the operator and the value on the right side of the operator and assigns the result to the variable on the left side of the operator
- ^=: Performs a bitwise XOR operation on the value on the left side of the operator and the value on the right side of the operator and assigns the result to the variable on the left side of the operator

Assignment operators can be used in a variety of ways. For example, you can use them to initialize variables, to update the values of variables, and to perform calculations. Here are some examples of how to use some of these assignment operators:

swift

```
// Initialize a variable
var count = 0
// Update the value of a variable
count += 1
// Perform a calculation
let sum = count + 1
// Assign the value of one variable to another variable
let anotherCount = count
```

It can be hard to remember that certain assignment operators that aren't often used exist, but they can save a lot of time and effort.

Basic Arithmetic Operations

Swift provides built-in operators for performing common arithmetic operations like addition, subtraction, multiplication, and division. The same symbols we were all taught in school are used for basic math in code and following similar rules to those we were taught.

Addition uses the + operator. In this example, a variable called sum will be filled with the result of 6 + 2, rather than 6 and 2, or the string of "6 + 2":

swift

```
let sum = 6 + 2
```

Subtraction works similarly, so we can create a variable called difference and allow it to be 10 minus 4, where the word minus is replaced with a - symbol:

swift

```
let difference = 10 - 4
```

Multiplication works the same, but instead of writing eleven times three, we use the integers and the * symbol:

swift

```
let product = 11 * 3
```

Division also works the same, but we can use the / instead of saying "12 over 3" or "12 divided by 3" as follows:

swift

```
let quotient = 12 / 3
```

Another common operation in code is to find the modulo, or remainder, where we'll use the % symbol:

swift

```
let remainder = 15 % 6
// remainder: 3
```

In the above examples, the basic arithmetic operations are performed and the results stored in variables. Swift follows the standard mathematical rules for operator precedence, which allow developers to write complex expressions involving multiple operations. Sometimes those can be done with one long line, but it's also good to break up more complex mathematical operations into separate lines or stanzas of code, either for readability or to group reusable bits together. We'll cover more complex mathematical operations later in the book, but in the meantime, we'll look at strings next.

String Manipulation

String manipulation involves modifying, combining, and extracting information from strings. Swift provides various methods and operators to manipulate strings effectively. Here are some common string manipulation operations:

Concatenation is joining two strings. The + operator is used to do so, as seen in the below concatenation of a name:

swift

```
let firstName = "Charles"
let lastName = "Edge"
let fullName = firstName + " " + lastName
```

In the above code, we concatenate the `firstName`, space, and `lastName` strings to form the `fullName` string using the + operator.

`String` interpolation is used to combine variables and constants with strings. Embed variables or expressions within a string using the \() syntax. In the following example, the value of updateFrequency is interpolated within the following message string:

swift

```
let updateFrequency = 30
let message = "We update every \(updateFrequency) days."
```

`String` Length is used to derive the length of a string. The count property retrieves the length of a string, which represents the number of characters in the string. The example below shows how to count the number of characters in a string called `computerName` by creating a string called `computerName` and then creating a variable called length that is populated using the .count property:

swift

```
let computerName = "Charles MacBook"
let length = computerName.count
```

`String` slicing extracts a substring from a string. This can be done in a number of ways, many of which involve various slicing properties. Let's take the prefix property as an example. The prefix property indexes a string and returns the first three characters of the string (if the 3 is provided in the parenthesis after the prefix property is called). For example:

swift

```
let IP = "192.168.50.1"
let firstOctet = IP.prefix(3)
```

This is similar to what the cut command does in bash or tcsh. However, Swift allows for much more complicated slicing. Take the .components property (which indicates the result will be an `Array`) - here it's straightforward to split each octet from that initial string by slicing each integer into an array separated by a ., as follows:

swift

```
let fullIP = IP.components(separatedBy: ".")
```

`String` modification is adding or removing information from a string. For example, the following example appends the string "Wi-fi" to the existing string "Corporate" to result in "Corporate Wi-fi" for the `wirelessNetwork` variable:

swift

```
var wirelessNetwork = "Corporate"
wirelessNetwork.append(contentsOf: " Wi-fi")
```

The `append(contentsOf:)` instance method adds new characters to the end of a collection (which in this case is an existing string).

Comparison Operators

One of the most important things software does is to compare one thing to another. This might be to check if a user is in a group, if an IP address is within a given range, or just if something is bigger than something else. Luckily, at the simplest level, the operators used to compare two objects use the same characters we learned in school. These are things like greater than symbols and less than symbols.

The way programming languages work, some comparison operators we learned in school are used for different tasks, like the equal sign, and so we use two to denote a comparison. This is one of the reasons that there are so many options for operators, which we'll cover in the next few sections.

Unary Operators

Unary operators operate on a single operand. They can be prefix or postfix, meaning that they can come before or after their operand. Prefix operators include the following: +, -, !, ~, and &. The main built-in postfix operator is: !.

Prefix operators come before their operand. For example, the following code shows how to use the prefix - operator to negate a number:

swift

```
let number = 10
let negativeNumber = -number
print(negativeNumber) // Outputs -10
```

Postfix operators come after their operand. For example, the following code shows how to use the postfix ! operator to "unwrap" an optional integer:

swift

```
let optionalCount: Int? = 12
let count = optionalCount!
print(optionalCount) // "Optional(12)"
print(count) // "12"
```

To perform a logical operation, use the ! as seen below:

swift

```
// Perform a logical operation
let isTrue = !false
```

Unary operators work with a single operand, but it's also possible to get more output, and so more options, with varying degrees of complexity, with ternary operators.

Ternary Conditional Operator

The ternary conditional operator is a three-operand operator that takes a boolean expression, a true value, and a false value and returns the true value if the expression is true or the false value if the expression is false. The ternary operator is written as follows, with a ? following the boolean expression and a : delimiting the next two:

swift

```
booleanExpression ? trueValue : falseValue
```

The boolean expression is evaluated first. If it evaluates to true, the `trueValue` is returned. If it evaluates to false, the `falseValue` is returned. The ternary operator can be used in a variety of ways. For example, it can be used to assign a value to a variable based on the result of an expression. It can also perform a calculation based on the result of an expression or return a different value from a function based on the result of an expression.

This first example assigns a value to a variable based on the result of an expression:

swift

```
let isTrue = true
let result = isTrue ? "True" : "False"
```

The next example performs a calculation based on the result of an expression:

swift

```
let number = 10
let nextNumber = number > 0 ? number + 1 : number - 1
```

It's also possible to return a different value from a function based on the result of an expression with a ternary conditional operator, as follows:

swift

```
func getGreeting() -> String {
  let timeOfDay = "Morning"
  return timeOfDay == "Morning" ? "Good morning!" : "Good evening!"
}
```

The ternary conditional operator worked with three objects. But variables needed to be filled. It's also possible to provide a default value at the time objects are substantiated, using nil-coalescing operators.

Nil-Coalescing Operator

The nil-coalescing operator, also known as the ?? operator, can be used to safely unwrap optionals and provide a default value if the optional is nil. It is a two-operand operator that takes an optional and a default value and returns the optional's value if it is not nil or the default value if the optional is nil.

The nil-coalescing operator can be used in a variety of ways. For example, it can safely unwrap an optional and provide a default value if the optional is nil. They can also assign a value to a variable based on the result of an optional or perform a calculation based on the result of an optional. They're also useful to return a different value from a function based on the result of an optional.

The nil-coalescing operator is written as follows:

swift

```
optional ?? defaultValue
```

The optional is evaluated first. If the optional is not nil, its value is returned. If the optional is nil, the `defaultValue` is returned. To safely unwrap an optional and provide the default value, simply define the variable, like name in the below example, and then the type followed by a = and the nil as the object:

swift

```
let name: String? = nil
let defaultName = "John Doe"
let unwrappedName = name ?? defaultName
```

To assign a value to a variable based on the result of the optional, you can then use it as seen in the if/else statement below:

swift

```
let greeting: String
if let name = name {
  greeting = "Hello, \(name)!"
} else {
  greeting = "Hello, stranger!"
}
```

or to perform a calculation based on the result:

swift

```
let number: Int? = 10
let incremented = (number ?? 0) + 1
```

or to return a different value from a function based on the result of the optional:

swift

```
func getGreeting() -> String? {
  let name: String? = nil
  return name ?? "Hello, stranger!"
}
```

The operators thus far can be used to manipulate various variables and compare the output. It's also possible to define a range of values (either for comparison or object storage). This is done with range operators.

Range Operators

Range operators define a range of values. They can be used to iterate over a range of values, to check if a value is within a range, and to perform other operations on ranges. There are two types of range operators: the closed range operator (...) and the half-open range operator (..<).

The closed range operator defines a range that includes all values from the lower bound to the upper bound. For example, the range 1...5 includes the values 1, 2, 3, 4, and 5. The half-open range operator defines a range that includes all values from the lower bound up to but not including the upper bound. For example, the range 1..<5 includes the values 1, 2, 3, and 4, but not 5.

Range operators can be used with a variety of types, including integers, floats, and dates. For example, to iterate over a range of values, use the ellipses in a for statement, as follows:

swift

```
for number in 1...5 {
  print(number)
}
```

To check if a value is within a range, use a comparison operator to get a boolean based on the range, as seen here:

swift

```
// Check if a value is within a range
let number = 3
let isWithinRange = 1...5 ~= number
```

Or to iterate to sum, use a stanza similar to the following:

swift

```
// Perform other operations on ranges
let range = 1...5
let sum = range.reduce(0, +)
```

Since the beginning of time, for programmers at least (if not since Aristotle invented logic as we know it today), there has been the concept of using AND with OR to string together powerful concepts. In programming, we call these logical operators.

Logical Operators

Logical operators are used to combine two or more logical expressions into a single logical expression. The result of a logical expression is a boolean value, which can be either true or false. Swift gives developers three standard logical operators:

- **Logical AND (&&)**: The logical AND operator returns true only if both operands are true.
- **Logical OR (||)**: The logical OR operator returns true if either operand is true.
- **Logical NOT (!)**: The logical NOT operator returns the opposite of its operand.

Logical operators can be used in a variety of ways. For example, they can be used to combine conditions in conditional statements, such as with the following if statement:

swift

```
if age >= 18 && hasDriversLicense {
  // The user can drive.
} else {
  // The user cannot drive.
}
```

Logical operators are also used to perform logical operations on data, such as checking if a value is within a certain range or if a string contains a certain substring:

swift

```
let string = "Hello, world!"
let isHelloWorld = string == "Hello, world!"
```

It's also possible to write more complex logical expressions, such as the following, which evaluates if a day of the week is Saturday or Sunday so we know how to route those tickets that come in when the software developers are out drinking, binge watching sci-fi, gaming, or enjoying nature (or whatever developers do when they aren't writing code):

swift

```
let isWeekend = (dayOfWeek == "Saturday" || dayOfWeek == "Sunday") &&
!isHoliday
```

Systems administrators need their weekends. That gives plenty of time to think of even more complex local operations - which are easily developed using compound assignment operators.

Compound Assignment Operators

Compound assignment operators in Swift allow you to perform a mathematical or logical operation on a variable and then assign the result back to the variable in one step. There are nine compound assignment operators in Swift:

- +=: Adds the value on the right side of the operator to the variable on the left side of the operator and assigns the result back to the variable on the left side of the operator
- -=: Subtracts the value on the right side of the operator from the variable on the left side of the operator and assigns the result back to the variable on the left side of the operator
- *=: Multiplies the value on the right side of the operator by the variable on the left side of the operator and assigns the result back to the variable on the left side of the operator
- /=: Divides the value on the left side of the operator by the value on the right side of the operator and assigns the result back to the variable on the left side of the operator

- %=: Divides the value on the left side of the operator by the value on the right side of the operator and assigns the remainder back to the variable on the left side of the operator
- <<=: Shifts the value on the left side of the operator to the left by the number of bits specified by the value on the right side of the operator and assigns the result back to the variable on the left side of the operator
- =: Shifts the value on the left side of the operator to the right by the number of bits specified by the value on the right side of the operator and assigns the result back to the variable on the left side of the operator
- &=: Performs a bitwise AND operation on the value on the left side of the operator and the value on the right side of the operator and assigns the result back to the variable on the left side of the operator
- |=: Performs a bitwise OR operation on the value on the left side of the operator and the value on the right side of the operator and assigns the result back to the variable on the left side of the operator
- ^=: Performs a bitwise XOR operation on the value on the left side of the operator and the value on the right side of the operator and assigns the result back to the variable on the left side of the operator

Compound assignment operators can be used in a variety of ways. One of the most common is to increment or decrement a variable by a certain amount. For example, to increment the variable count by one, use the += to set the new value one higher, as seen here:

swift

```
var count = 0
count += 1
```

It's also possible to add or subtract two values and assign the result to a variable. The following operation performs a simple mathematical function and then subtracts two more from the value of the difference variable:

swift

```
var difference = 10 - 5
difference -= 2
```

Addition and subtraction are one mathematical operation, but it's also possible to multiply or divide two values and assign the result to a variable, as follows:

swift

```
var product = 5 * 6
product *= 2
```

or to use division:

swift

```
var quotient = 10 / 5
quotient /= 2
```

Finally, &= can be used to perform boolean logic operations on two values and assign the result to a variable:

swift

```
var isTrue = true
isTrue &= false
```

Without the advent of more and more cryptographic work, such as using passkeys and SSO extensions, there's been a renewed need to do work on bitwise operators as well.

Bitwise Operators

Bitwise operators are a special type of operator that operate on individual bits of data. They can be used to perform a variety of operations, such as setting, clearing, or toggling bits. Bitwise operators are often used in low-level programming, such as graphics programming and device driver creation, but they can also be useful for more general-purpose programming tasks.

There are six bitwise operators in Swift:

- &: Bitwise AND (&) performs a bitwise AND operation on two operands. The result of a bitwise AND operation is a bit that is 1 if both operands are 1, and 0 otherwise.

- |: Bitwise OR (|) performs a bitwise OR operation on two operands. The result of a bitwise OR operation is a bit that is 1 if either operand is 1, and 0 otherwise.
- ^: Bitwise XOR (^) performs a bitwise XOR operation on two operands. The result of a bitwise XOR operation is a bit that is 1 if one operand is 1 and the other operand is 0, and 0 otherwise.
- <<: Bitwise left shift (<<) shifts the bits of an operand to the left by the number of places specified by the other operand. The bits that are shifted off the left side of the operand are discarded.
- >>: Bitwise right shift (>>) shifts the bits of an operand to the right by the number of places specified by the other operand. The bits that are shifted off the right side of the operand are discarded.
- ~: Bitwise NOT (~) performs a bitwise NOT operation on an operand. The result of a bitwise NOT operation is a bit that is the opposite of the corresponding bit in the operand.

Bitwise operators can be used to set or clear individual bits of data. For example, set the first bit of a variable, with the UInt9 flag:

swift

```
var flags: UInt8 = 0
flags |= 1 << 0
```

or clear the fifth bit of a variable:

swift

```
flags &= ~(1 << 4)
```

or simply toggle the fifth bit of a variable:

swift

```
flags ^= 1 << 4
```

or comparisons, like check if the seventh bit of a variable is set:

swift

```
let isSixthBitSet = (flags & (1 << 6)) != 0
```

or implement low-level algorithms, such as to reverse bits of a byte:

swift

```
func reverseBits(_ byte: UInt8) -> UInt8 {
  var reversedByte: UInt8 = 0
  for i in 0..<8 {
    reversedByte |= (byte & (1 << (7 - i))) >> i
  }
  return reversedByte
}
```

Twiddling bits is one lower-level operation developers perform. Another is when writing code to put a value that is too large or too small into an existing binary space. This is when overflow operators are commonly used.

Overflow Operators

Overflow operators are used to perform arithmetic operations on integers without checking for overflow. This can be useful for certain types of applications, such as low-level programming and graphics programming. However, it is important to use overflow operators with caution, as they can lead to unexpected results if the operands are too large or too small.

There are three overflow operators in Swift:

- &+: Overflow addition
- &-: Overflow subtraction
- &*: Overflow multiplication

These operators are similar to the regular arithmetic operators, but they do not check for overflow. This means that if the result of an operation is too large or too small for the data type of the operands, the result will be wrapped around to the next possible value.

For example, the following code will overflow the `Int` data type:

swift

```
var number: Int = Int.max
number &+ 1 // This will result in the value -1
```

This is because the maximum value for the `Int` data type is `Int.max`, and adding 1 to `Int.max` will result in a value that is too large for the `Int` data type. Therefore, the result is wrapped around to the next possible value, which is -1. A more elegant approach might be to simply split the operation up and add a sanity check and logic to deal with the fact that the value is out of bounds in a more intentional fashion.

Operator Precedence

Operator precedence is a set of rules that determines the order in which operators are evaluated in an expression. This is important because it affects the result of the expression. This is similar to the PEMDAS order of operations for math that many kids learn in gradeschool, but applied to programming. In general, operators with higher precedence are evaluated first, then they are evaluated from left to right, and parentheses are used to override the normal order of evaluation.

For example, the expression 1 + 2 * 3 will evaluate to 7, not 9. This is because multiplication has higher precedence than addition. Therefore, the multiplication operation is performed first, resulting in the value 6. Then, the addition operation is performed, resulting in the final value of 7.

Here is a table of operator precedence in Swift:

```
| Precedence | Operators |
|---|---|---|
| Highest | (), ->, ., ?, ! |
| Higher | +, -, *, /, % |
| | <<, >> |
| | &, |, ^ |
| | ==, !=, <, >, <=, >= |
| | && |
| | || |
| Lowest | =, +=, -=, *=, /=, %=, <<=, >>=, &=, |=, ^=, where |
```

Use parentheses to override the normal order of evaluation. For example, the expression (1 + 2) * 3 will evaluate to 9, not 7. This is because the parentheses force the addition operation to be performed first.

Operator Methods

Operator methods are used to define custom implementations of existing operators for your own types. This can be useful for making your code more concise and expressive. To define an operator method, you simply need to declare a static method on your type with the same name as the operator you want to overload. The method must take two arguments.

For example, the following code defines an operator method for the Point struct:

swift

```
struct Point {
  var x: Int
  var y: Int
  static func +(_ lhs: Point, _ rhs: Point) -> Point {
    return Point(x: lhs.x + rhs.x, y: lhs.y + rhs.y)
  }
}
```

This operator method allows us to add two Point values together using the + operator. For example, the following code will print the point (3, 5):

swift

```
let point1 = Point(x: 1, y: 2)
let point2 = Point(x: 2, y: 3)
let sum = point1 + point2
print(sum)
```

Operator methods can be used to overload any of the built-in operators in Swift. This includes arithmetic operators, logical operators, comparison operators, and assignment operators.

Custom Operators

Custom operators can also be used in Swift. This can be a useful way to add new functionality to your code or to make your code more concise. To create a custom operator, first you must declare the operator itself:

swift

```
infix operator <->
```

The operator must be declared as either `infix`, `prefix`, or `postfix`. Infix operators are used between two operands, prefix operators are used in front of a single operand, and postfix operators are used after a single operand.

After having defined the operator, the function must be defined. The name of the function must be the same as the operator that you want to create, and the parameters must match the type of operator.

For example, the following code allows our custom <-> operator to be used to compare the first three characters of two strings:

swift

```
func <-> (lhs: String, rhs: String) -> Bool {
  return lhs.prefix(3) == rhs.prefix(3)
}
```

This function takes two strings as operands and returns a boolean value. The function compares the two strings and returns true if they have the same first three characters. Once you have defined a custom operator, you can use it in your code. For example:

swift

```
let string1 = "Hello"
let string2 = "Helicopter"
if string1 <-> string2 {
  print("The strings have the same prefix.")
} else {
  print("The strings do not have the same prefix.")
}
```

In this example, we compare the strings string1 and string2 using the <-> operator. If the strings have the same prefix, the code will print the message "The strings have the same prefix." Otherwise, the code will print the message "The strings do not have the same prefix."

Substrings

Substrings are slices of strings. They can represent a portion of a string, or even the entire string itself. Substrings are created using the subscript operator or using the `prefix()`, `suffix()`, and `split()` methods. Substrings can be used in a variety of ways, such as

- To extract a portion of a string for further processing
- To compare two strings to see if they have the same prefix or suffix
- To split a string into an array of substrings
- To create a new string by combining multiple substrings

To get a substring from a string using the subscript operator, you simply need to pass the start and end indices of the substring to the operator. The start index is the index of the first character in the substring, and the end index is the index of the character after the last character in the substring. For example:

swift

```
let str = "Hello, World!"
let startIndex = str.startIndex
let endIndex = str.index(startIndex, offsetBy: 5)
let substring = str[startIndex ..< endIndex]
print(substring) // "Hello"
```

The previous example could also have been achieved using simply the `prefix()` method:

swift

```
let str = "Hello, World!"
print(str.prefix(5))
```

The `prefix()` and `suffix()` methods can be used to get the prefix or suffix of a string, respectively. The `split()` method can be used to split a string into an array of substrings, using a specified separator.

For example, the following code will split the string “Hello, world!” into an array of two substrings, “Hello” and “world!”:

swift

```
let greeting = "Hello, world!"
let splitGreeting = greeting.split(separator: ",")
print(splitGreeting) // Prints ["Hello", " world!"]
```

It's also possible to compare the two earlier substrings to check that they match. For example, the following will evaluate the prefix of string1 and string2 and print the result:

swift

```
let string1 = "Hello, world!"
let string2 = "Hello, everyone!"
if string1.prefix(5) == string2.prefix(5) {
  print("The two strings have the same prefix")
}
if string1.suffix(6) == string2.suffix(6) {
  print("The two strings have the same suffix")
}
```

It's also possible to split a string into an array of substrings, as follows:

swift

```
let greeting = "Hello, world!"
let splitGreeting = greeting.split(separator: ",")
// Create a new string by combining multiple substrings
let firstName = "John"
let lastName = "Doe"
let fullName = firstName + " " + lastName
print(fullName) // Prints "John Doe"
```

Substrings are one way to match for a pattern, but for more complex patterns, look to regular expressions.

Regular Expressions

Regular expressions, also known as regex, are used to search, edit, and manipulate text. They can be used to find patterns in text, replace text, and validate input. Regular expressions are made up of a sequence of characters that define a search pattern. The characters in a regular expression can be literal characters, special characters, or metacharacters.

Literal characters are simply the characters that they represent. For example, the literal character "a" matches the character "a". Special characters have special meaning in regular expressions. For example, the special character "." matches any character. Metacharacters are used to define complex patterns. For example, the metacharacter * matches zero or more of the previous character.

Swift has a `Regex` type (Swift 5.7 and later). You typically create a regex and then use methods on `String` like `matches(of:)`, `firstMatch(of:)`, and `replacing(_:with:)`.

Here is an example of how to use regular expressions in Swift to find all occurrences of the word "hello" in a string:

swift

```
let string = "Hello, world!"
let regex = try! Regex("Hello")
let matches = string.matches(of: regex)
for match in matches {
  print(match.0)
}
```

This code will print the following output:

swift

```
Hello
```

You can also use regular expressions to replace text in a string. For example, the following code will replace all occurrences of the word "hello" with the word "hi":

swift

```
let string = "Hello, world!"
let regex = try! Regex("Hello")
let updatedString = string.replacing(regex, with: "Hi")
print(updatedString)
```

This code will print the following output:

swift

```
Hi, world!
```

Regular expressions are important for any developer, but the ability to match patterns quickly and efficiently is even more important for systems administrators than most, where we're often parsing through logs, json files, and defaults domains. Note that regular expressions may take some time to get the hang of, as with great power can come great complexity.

Special Characters in String Literals

Special characters in string literals are characters that have a special meaning to the compiler. They can be used to escape characters, to represent non-ASCII characters, and to perform other tasks. There are two types of special characters in string literals: escape characters and Unicode scalars.

Escape characters are used to escape special characters, such as the newline character (\n) and the double quotation mark ("). They are also used to represent non-ASCII characters, such as the copyright symbol (©) and the euro symbol (€). Unicode scalars are used to represent non-ASCII characters using their hexadecimal code points. For example, the Unicode scalar for the copyright symbol is \u{00A9}.

To use a special character in a string literal, you simply need to precede it with a backslash (\). For example, the following string literal contains an escape character for the newline character:

swift

```
"This is the first line\nThis is the second line"
```

This string literal will be printed on two lines, with the second line starting on a new line.

The following string literal contains a Unicode scalar for the copyright symbol:

swift

```
"This is a copyrighted work © 2023"
```

This string literal will be printed with the copyright symbol at the end of the sentence. Special characters are common, but it's also useful to treat multiple lines as literals in the same fashion when multiple special characters appear.

Multiline String Literals

Multiline string literals in Swift are a way to create strings that span multiple lines. They can be used to make your code more readable and maintainable, especially when working with large or complex strings. These are helpful to create documentation strings and error messages.

To create a multiline string literal, you simply need to surround the string with three double quotation marks (""""). For example, the following code creates a multiline string literal:

swift

```
"""
This is a multiline string literal.
It can span multiple lines.
"""
```

When you print a multiline string literal, Swift preserves the contents of the string. However, it does provide indentation handling: the indentation of the closing delimiter is used to determine how much indentation to strip from each line.

Here are some examples of how to use multiline string literals:

swift

```
/// This function does something.
func myFunction() {
  // ...
}
// Create an error message
let errorMessage = """
An unexpected error occurred.
Please try again later.
"""
// Create code that is more readable and maintainable
```

```
let html = """
<!DOCTYPE html>
<html>
<head>
  <title>My Web Page</title>
</head>
<body>
  <h1>Welcome to my web page!</h1>
</body>
</html>
"""
```

Multiline string literals are useful for a number of tasks. For example, Jamf extension attributes use an eerily similar structure as the above function.

String Delimiters

String delimiters are characters (or sequences of characters) used to separate text into smaller parts. In Swift, this is most commonly done by using a separator character with methods like split(separator:). For more complex parsing and pattern matching, you can use regular expressions.

Literal delimiters are specific characters used to separate strings. For example, the comma character (,) is a common delimiter used to separate items in a list.

Here are some examples of how to use string delimiters:

swift

```
// Use a literal delimiter to split a string into an array of substrings
let string = "This,is,a,comma-separated,list"
let listItems = string.split(separator: ",")
for item in listItems {
  print(item)
}
// Output:
// This
// is
// a
```

```
// comma-separated
// list
// Use a regex pattern to extract all URLs from a string
let string = "This string contains several URLs: https://www.google.com,
https://www.apple.com, and https://www.microsoft.com"
let regex = try! Regex("https?://\\w+\\.\\w+")
let matches = string.matches(of: regex)
for match in matches {
  print(match.0)
}
// Output:
// https://www.google.com
// https://www.apple.com
// https://www.microsoft.com
```

String Mutability

String mutability in Swift refers to the ability to change the value of a string variable. String variables are declared either as mutable (using var) or immutable (using let). String mutability is useful for editing text, building strings dynamically, and validating input. Mutable string variables can be changed after they are declared. For example, the following code declares a mutable string variable name and then changes its value:

swift

```
var name = "John Doe"
name = "Jane Doe"
print(name) // Prints "Jane Doe"
```

Immutable string variables cannot be changed after they are declared. For example, the following code will cause a compile-time error:

swift

```
let name = "John Doe"
name = "Jane Doe" // Compile-time error
```

Concatenating Strings

String concatenation in Swift is the process of joining two or more strings together. There are two main ways to concatenate strings in Swift: using the + operator and using the append() method.

The + operator can be used to concatenate two strings of any type. To do this, simply place the strings you want to concatenate on either side of the + operator. For example, the following code concatenates the strings "Hello" and "world!":

swift

```
let greeting = "Hello" + " world!"
print(greeting) // Prints "Hello world!"
```

You can also use the + operator to concatenate multiple strings together. For example, the following code concatenates the strings "Hello", "world", and "!":

swift

```
let greeting = "Hello" + " world!" + "!"
print(greeting) // Prints "Hello world!"
```

Use the append() method to concatenate a string to the end of a mutable string variable. To do this, simply call the append() method on the string variable and pass in the string you want to append. For example, the following code appends the string "world!" to the end of the string variable greeting:

swift

```
var greeting = "Hello"
greeting.append(" world!")
print(greeting) // Prints "Hello world!"
```

You can also use the append() method to append multiple strings to the end of a mutable string variable. For example, the following code appends the strings "world" and "!" to the end of the string variable greeting:

swift

```
var greeting = "Hello"
greeting.append(" world!")
greeting.append("!")
print(greeting) // Prints "Hello world!"
```

Which method you use to concatenate strings in Swift depends on your specific needs. If you are concatenating two or more strings together and you do not need to modify the original strings, then you should use the + operator. If you are concatenating a string to the end of a mutable string variable, then you should use the `append()` method.

Interpolating Strings

`String` interpolation allows developers to embed variables and expressions within strings. This can be useful for creating dynamic strings, such as error messages, log messages, and user interfaces. To interpolate a variable or expression into a string, you simply place it inside parentheses and precede it with a backslash (\). For example, the following code interpolates the variable name into the string "Hello, (name)!":

swift

```
let name = "Alice"
let greeting = "Hello, \(name)!"
print(greeting) // Prints "Hello, Alice!"
```

You can also interpolate expressions into strings. For example, the following code interpolates the expression 1 + 2 into the string "The sum is (1 + 2)":

swift

```
let message = "The sum is \(1 + 2)"
print(message) // Prints "The sum is 3"
```

`String` interpolation can be used to interpolate any type of value into a string, including variables, constants, expressions, and objects. One use of such interpolation might be to encode string data into other formats.

Encoding

Encoding is the process of converting values within a running program into a format that can be stored or transmitted. This can be done for a variety of reasons, such as to save space, to improve performance, or to make the data more portable. There are plenty of encoding formats available, but some of the most common ones include

- **JSON**: JSON is a text-based encoding format that is commonly used for exchanging data between web applications.
- **Property lists (PLISTs)**: PLISTs are a binary encoding format that is often used to store application settings and data.
- **XML**: XML is a markup language that is commonly used to represent and exchange data.
- **UTF-8**: UTF-8 is a character encoding that is used to represent text in most modern computer systems.

To encode data into formats that are known, use the Encoder protocol. The Encoder protocol provides a number of methods for encoding different types of data, such as strings, numbers, arrays, and dictionaries:

- To encode a value to JSON, you can use the JSONEncoder class. The JSONEncoder class implements the Encoder protocol and provides a number of methods for encoding different types of data to JSON.
- To encode a value to a PLIST, you can use the PropertyListEncoder class. The PropertyListEncoder class implements the Encoder protocol and provides a number of methods for encoding different types of data to PLISTs.
- XML encoding is not built into Swift, but there are several open source Swift packages which provide an XMLEncoder type.
- To encode a string to UTF-8, you can use the `String.data(_:using:)` method. The `String.data(_:using:)` method returns a data object that contains the string encoded using the given encoding.

The following sections cover a few of these in more detail.

Showing a String As Unicode

Unicode is a standard encoding system that represents characters from almost all languages. Every Unicode character is encoded using a unique integer code point between 0 and 0x10FFFF. To show a string as Unicode, use the `unicodeScalars` property of the `String` type.

The `unicodeScalars` property returns a collection of UnicodeScalar values, which represent the individual Unicode characters in the string. To iterate over the `unicodeScalars` property, you can use a for-in loop. For example, the following code prints the Unicode code point for each character in the string "Hello, world!":

swift

```
let string = "Hello, world!"
for unicodeScalar in string.unicodeScalars {
  print(unicodeScalar.value)
}
```

This code will produce the following output:

swift

```
72
101
108
108
111
32
119
101
114
108
100
33
```

You can also use the `unicodeScalars` property to generate a string representation of the Unicode code points for each character in a string. To do this, you can use the `map()` method to convert the UnicodeScalar values in the `unicodeScalars` property to strings. For example, the following code generates a string representation of the Unicode code points for each character in the string "Hello, world!":

swift

```
let string = "Hello, world!"
let unicodeCodePoints = string.unicodeScalars.map { String($0.value) }
let unicodeString = unicodeCodePoints.joined(separator: "")
print(unicodeString)
```

This code will produce the following output:

swift

```
\u0048\u0065\u006C\u006C\u006F\u0020\u0077\u006F\u0072\u006C\u0064\u0021
```

This string representation is one way to display these scalars. Another is to show actual values.

Showing a String As a Unicode Scalar

A Unicode scalar is a single Unicode character. Unicode scalars are encoded using a unique integer code point between 0 and 0x10FFFF. To show a string as a Unicode scalar in Swift, you can use the `unicodeScalars` property of the `String` type. The `unicodeScalars` property returns a collection of UnicodeScalar values, which represent the individual Unicode characters in the string.

To access the Unicode scalar for a specific character in a string, you can use the subscript operator. For example, the following code gets the Unicode scalar for the first character in the string "Hello, world!":

swift

```
let string = "Hello, world!"
let firstUnicodeScalar = string.unicodeScalars.first!
print(firstUnicodeScalar.value) // Prints 72
```

The value property of the UnicodeScalar type returns the integer code point for the Unicode scalar. The `unicodeScalars` property can also generate a string representation of the Unicode scalar for a specific character in a string. Use the description property of the UnicodeScalar type. For example, the following code generates a string representation of the Unicode scalar for the first character in the string "Hello, world!":

swift

```
let string = "Hello, world!"
let firstUnicodeScalarString = string.unicodeScalars.first!.description
print(firstUnicodeScalarString) // Prints "\u0048"
```

This string representation of the Unicode scalar can be useful for debugging purposes or for sharing Unicode scalars with other systems. Remember to use the subscript operator to access the Unicode scalar for a specific character in a string. Also use the description property of the UnicodeScalar type to generate a string representation of the Unicode scalar.

Showing a String As UTF-16

UTF-16 is a character encoding scheme that uses 16-bit code units to represent Unicode characters. UTF-16 is the most commonly used character encoding scheme in Swift. To show a string as UTF-16 in Swift, use the utf16 property of the `String` type. The utf16 property returns a collection of `UInt16` values, which represent the UTF-16 code units for the Unicode characters in the string.

To iterate over the utf16 property, you can use a for-in loop. For example, the following code prints the UTF-16 code unit for each character in the string "Hello, world!":

swift

```
let string = "Hello, world!"
for utf16CodeUnit in string.utf16 {
  print(utf16CodeUnit)
}
```

This code will produce the following output:

swift

```
72
101
108
108
111
32
119
101
114
108
100
33
```

You can also use the utf16 property to generate a byte representation of the UTF-16 code units for a string. To do this, you can use the `withUnsafeBytes()` method to access the bytes of the `UInt16` values in the utf16 property. For example, the following code generates a byte representation of the UTF-16 code units for the string "Hello, world!":

swift

```
let string = "Hello, world!"
var utf16Bytes = [UInt8]()
string.utf16.withUnsafeBytes { (buffer: UnsafeBufferPointer<UInt16>) in
  utf16Bytes = Array(buffer)
}
print(utf16Bytes)
```

This code will produce the following output:

swift

```
[72, 0, 101, 0, 108, 0, 108, 0, 111, 0, 32, 0, 119, 0, 101, 0, 114, 0, 108,
0, 100, 0, 33]
```

This byte representation of the UTF-16 code units can be useful for debugging purposes or for sharing UTF-16 strings with other systems.

Counting Characters

Counting characters in Swift is a simple task that can be performed using the count property on the `String` type. The count property returns the number of characters in the string.

For example, the following code counts the number of characters in the string "Hello, world!":

swift

```
let string = "Hello, world!"
let characterCount = string.count
print(characterCount) // Prints 13
```

This code will produce the following output:

swift

```
13
```

You can also use the count property to count the number of characters in a specific range of a string. To do this, first extract the range via subscript and then access the count property on the returned substring. For example, the following code counts the number of characters in the range from the start of the string to the space character:

swift

```
let string = "Hello, world!"
let characterCount = string[string.startIndex..<string.firstIndex(of: "
")!].count
print(characterCount) // Prints 6
```

This code will produce the following output:

swift

```
6
```

The encoded data is one form of a string. A common task with those strings is to compare them.

Comparing Strings

Comparing strings in Swift is a simple task that can be performed using the equality operator (==) or the inequality operators (!=, <, >, <=, >=). The equality operator (==) returns true if the two strings are equal and false if they are not equal. For example, the following code compares the strings "Hello, world!" and "Hello, world!":

swift

```
let string1 = "Hello, world!"
let string2 = "Hello, world!"
if string1 == string2 {
  print("The strings are equal.")
} else {
  print("The strings are not equal.")
}
```

This code will produce the following output:

swift

```
The strings are equal.
```

The inequality operators (!=, <, >, <=, >=) return true if the two strings are not equal and false if they are equal. For example, the following code compares the strings "Hello, world!" and "Hello, world! again!":

swift

```
let string1 = "Hello, world!"
let string2 = "Hello, world! again!"
if string1 != string2 {
  print("The strings are not equal.")
} else {
  print("The strings are equal.")
}
```

This code will produce the following output:

swift

```
The strings are not equal.
```

Inequality operators can also compare strings lexicographically. This means that the strings are compared character by character, starting at the beginning of the strings. For example, the following code compares the strings "Hello, world!" and "Hello, world! again!":

swift

```
let string1 = "Hello, world!"
let string2 = "Hello, world! again!"
if string1 < string2 {
  print("The first string is less than the second string.")
} else if string1 > string2 {
  print("The first string is greater than the second string.")
} else {
  print("The strings are equal.")
}
```

This code will produce the following output:

swift

```
The first string is less than the second string.
```

Comparing strings to one another is a common enough task. Another is to convert variables from one type to another.

Type Casting and Inheritance

Type casting allows developers to convert a variable or constant from one type to another. Inheritance allows developers to create a new type that inherits from an existing type. Type casting can be used to convert a variable or constant from one type to another. As of the time of this writing, there are two types of type casting available: upcasting and downcasting.

Upcasting is the process of converting a variable or constant from a more specific type to a more general type. For example, you could upcast a variable of type `Dog` to a variable of type `Animal`. Downcasting is the process of converting a variable or constant from a more general type to a more specific type. For example, you could downcast a variable of type `Animal` to a variable of type `Dog`. To upcast a variable or constant, you simply use the as keyword. For example, the following code upcasts a variable of type `Dog` to a variable of type `Animal`:

swift

```
let dog = Dog(name: "Fido")
let animal = dog as Animal
```

To downcast a variable or constant, you use the as? keyword. The as? keyword returns an optional value, which means that it could be nil if the downcast is not possible. For example, the following code downcasts a variable of type `Animal` to a variable of type `Dog`:

swift

```
let animal = Animal(name: "Fido")
let dog = animal as? Dog
if let dog = dog {
  // The downcast was successful.
} else {
  // The downcast was not successful.
}
```

Inheritance allows you to create a new type that inherits from an existing type. This means that the new type will inherit all of the properties and methods of the existing type.

To create a new type that inherits from an existing type, you use the class keyword and the : operator. For example, the following code creates a new type called Dog that inherits from the existing type Animal:

swift

```
class Dog: Animal {
  // ...
}
```

The Dog type inherits all of the properties and methods of the Animal type. This means that you can create instances of the Dog type and use them in the same way that you would create and use instances of the Animal type.

Type casting and inheritance can be used together to create powerful and flexible code. For example, the following code uses type casting to check the type of an instance and then call the appropriate method:

swift

```
class Animal {
  func speak() {
    print("Animal noise")
  }
}
class Dog: Animal {
  let name: String
  init(name: String) { self.name = name }
  override func speak() {
    print("Woof!")
  }
  func wagTail() {
    print("(Dog wagged tail)")
  }
}
let animal: Animal = Dog(name: "Fido")
animal.speak()
```

```
if let dog = animal as? Dog {
  dog.wagTail()
}
```

This code will print the following output:

swift

```
Woof!
(Dog wagged tail)
```

Checking Types

There are two ways to check types in Swift: using the `is` keyword and using the `type(of:)` function. The `is` keyword returns true if the value on the left-hand side of the operator is an instance of the type on the right-hand side of the operator. Otherwise, the is operator returns false.

For example, the following code checks if the value of the variable animal is an instance of the type Dog:

swift

```
let animal: Animal = Dog(name: "Fido")
if animal is Dog {
  print("The animal is a dog.")
} else {
  print("The animal is not a dog.")
}
```

This code will print the following output:

swift

```
The animal is a dog.
```

The `type(of:)` function returns the type of the value passed to the function. For example, the following code gets the type of the variable animal and stores it in the variable type:

swift

```
let animal = Dog(name: "Fido")
let type = type(of: animal)
print(type)
```

This code will print the following output:

swift

```
Dog
```

The `type(of:)` function is mostly useful for debugging purposes. For example, if your animal is quacking but you thought it was a dog, you can check if the problem is that there is a bug in Dog that makes dogs quack or if a bug somewhere else has caused you to be unexpectedly dealing with a duck.

swift

```
func makeAnimalSpeak(animal: Animal) {
  print("Debugging animal of type \(type(of: animal))")
  animal.speak()
}
```

Downcasting

Downcasting in Swift is the process of converting a variable or constant from a more general type to a more specific type. For example, you could downcast a variable of type `Animal` to a variable of type Dog.

Downcasting can be useful for accessing the specific properties and methods of a more specific type. For example, if you have a variable of type `Animal`, you can downcast it to a variable of type Dog in order to call the `bark()` method.

To downcast a variable or constant, you use the as? keyword. The as? keyword returns an optional value, which means that it could be nil if the downcast is not possible. For example, the following code downcasts a variable of type `Animal` to a variable of type Dog:

swift

```
let animal: Animal = Dog(name: "Fido")
if let dog = animal as? Dog {
  // The downcast was successful.
  dog.bark()
} else {
  // The downcast was not successful.
}
```

The if let statement is used to check if the downcast was successful. If the downcast was successful, the dog variable will contain a valid instance of the Dog type and you can call the bark() method. If the downcast was not successful, the dog variable will be unable to be created, and the code will take the else branch instead.

Type Nesting

Type nesting in Swift is the ability to define one type inside of another type. This can be useful for organizing your code and making it more readable and maintainable. The following code shows an example of type nesting:

swift

```
struct Card {
  var suit: Suit
  var rank: Int
  enum Suit {
    case spades
    case hearts
    case diamonds
    case clubs
  }
}
```

In this example, we have a Suit enum nested inside of the Card struct. This means that the Card struct can only have a Suit value for its suit property. We can use type nesting to create more complex types. For example, the following code shows a nested type that represents a deck of cards:

swift

```
struct Deck {
  var cards: Cards
  typealias Cards = [Card]
}
```

The Deck struct has a nested type called Cards, which is an array of Card structs. This means that the Deck struct can only contain Card structs in its cards property.

Extensions

An extension is used to add new functionality to an existing type, such as a class, struct, enumeration, or protocol. Extensions can be used to add new properties, methods, initializers, and subscripts to an existing type. This adds functionality without the need to modify the type itself, especially useful when trying to extend the functionality of a type that is defined by a framework, library, or other module - and so cannot be modified. They can also be useful to group related bits of functionality together.

Extensions can add the following new functionality to an existing type:

- Computed properties
- Instance methods and type methods
- Initializers
- Subscripts
- Nested types
- Conformance to protocols

Extensions can also be used to override existing methods and properties, but this is generally not recommended. To create an extension in Swift, you use the extension keyword followed by the name of the type that you want to extend:

swift

```
extension MyType {
    // Add new functionality to MyType here.
}
```

For example, the following extension adds a new property called `myProperty` to the `String` type:

swift

```
extension String {
    var myProperty: String {
        return "This is my property."
    }
}
```

Now it's possible to access the `myProperty` property on any string variable:

swift

```
let myString = "Hello, world!"
print(myString.myProperty) // Prints "This is my property."
```

Keep in mind that extensions can only add new functionality to existing types. Avoid using extensions to modify or override the behavior of existing methods or properties. Also document extensions clearly (including why they were created) so that other developers can understand them.

Computed Type Properties

Computed type properties are a type of property that can be calculated on the fly. They are similar to computed instance properties, but they are declared at the type level rather than the instance level. This means that they can be accessed without creating an instance of the type.

To declare a computed type property, you use the static keyword followed by the var keyword, the property name, a colon, and the type that will be returned. Then, you provide a getter closure that calculates the value of the property.

For example, the following code declares a computed type property called `greatestCommonDivisor` on the `Int` type:

swift

```
extension Int {
  static var greatestCommonDivisor: Int {
    return 1
  }
}
```

The `greatestCommonDivisor` property returns the greatest common divisor of all integers:

swift

```
print(Int.greatestCommonDivisor) // Prints 1
```

CHAPTER 3

Control Flow and Conditional Statements

Variables, types, and constants represent the ability to store information programmatically. Next, software developers need to move data. Statements allow developers to group expressions and so more easily control aspects of the order of execution. Statements can be used to perform tasks, to make decisions, and to repeat blocks of code.

There are many different types of statements in Swift. Some of the most common statements include assignment, expression, control flow, function calls, and return statements. We'll go through each in this section. Assignment statements are used to assign values to variables. For example:

swift

```
var x = 10
let y = 20
x = y
```

Expression statements are used to evaluate expressions. For example:

swift

```
let z = x + y
```

Control flow statements are used to make decisions and to repeat blocks of code. For example:

swift

```
if x > y {
  print("x is greater than y.")
} else {
```


C. Edge et al., *Mastering Swift*, https://doi.org/10.1007/979-8-8688-2770-9_3

```
  print("y is greater than x.")
}
while x < 100 {
  x = x + 1
}
```

Function calls are used to call functions. For example:

swift

```
func factorial(of number: Int) -> Int {
  if number == 0 {
    return 1
  } else {
    return number * factorial(of: number - 1)
  }
}
let factorialOf5 = factorial(of: 5)
```

Return statements are used to return values from functions. For example:

swift

```
func factorial(of number: Int) -> Int {
  if number == 0 {
    return 1
  } else {
    return number * factorial(of: number - 1)
  }
}
let factorialOf5 = factorial(of: 5)
print(factorialOf5) // 120
```

If-Else Statements and Their Syntax

Conditional statements play a crucial role in controlling the flow of your code. One of the most commonly used conditional statements is the if-else statement, which allows you to execute different blocks of code based on certain conditions. The basic syntax of an if-else statement in Swift is as follows:

swift

```
if condition {
    // Code to be executed if the condition is true
} else {
    // Code to be executed if the condition is false
}
```

In the above syntax, the condition is an expression that evaluates to either true or false. If the condition is true, the code block within the if statement is executed. If the condition is false, the code block within the else statement is executed.

The if statement can be used alone without an else statement. In this case, if the condition is true, the code block within the if statement is executed. If the condition is false, the code block is skipped.

swift

```
if condition {
    // Code to be executed if the condition is true
}
```

Most developers will want one thing to happen if a condition is true and another thing to happen if the condition is false, thus the need for not only if but also if-else. But other statements can be nested inside the if or else.

Multiple Conditions with Else-If

You can chain multiple conditions using else-if statements to test for different possibilities. The else-if statements are evaluated sequentially until a condition evaluates to true. Once a true condition is found, the corresponding code block is executed, and the rest of the else-if and else statements are skipped.

swift

```
if condition1 {
    // Code to be executed if condition1 is true
} else if condition2 {
```

```
    // Code to be executed if condition2 is true
} else {
    // Code to be executed if all conditions are false
}
```

If-else statements can be nested within each other to handle more complex conditions. This allows you to perform multiple levels of condition checking.

swift

```
if condition1 {
    if condition2 {
        // Code to be executed if both condition1 and condition2 are true
    } else {
        // Code to be executed if condition1 is true and condition2
is false
    }
} else {
    // Code to be executed if condition1 is false
}
```

There's also often the need to only do an operation if several conditions are met without nesting all the if-then logic.

Boolean Expressions in Conditions

The condition in an if-else statement must be a boolean expression that evaluates to either true or false. This can be achieved using comparison operators (e.g., ==, !=, >, <, >=, <=), logical operators (e.g., && for AND, || for OR, ! for NOT), or any other expression that returns a boolean value. For example, to check that the value of x is greater than y AND that z is 0, the following could be used:

swift

```
if x > y && z == 0 {
    // Code to be executed if x is greater than y and z is equal to 0
}
```

This allows further logic than if this one thing is true then do a certain operation; otherwise, do this other operation, unless something else is true. There's also shorthand (or ternary conditional operators) to write simpler if-thens, which can actually be easier to read.

Ternary Conditional Operator

Use the ternary conditional operator ? : as a shorthand for simple if-else statements. It has the following syntax:

swift

```
condition ? expression1 : expression2
```

If the condition is true, `expression1` is evaluated and returned. If the condition is false, `expression2` is evaluated and returned.

swift

```
let result = condition ? value1 : value2
```

In the above code, if the condition is true, `value1` is assigned to `result`; otherwise, `value2` is assigned. However, we can get far more detailed with how we compare objects to one another with even more operators.

Comparison and Logical Operators

In Swift, a powerful and modern programming language developed by Apple, comparison and logical operators are essential tools for evaluating conditions and making decisions in your code. These operators allow you to compare values, combine conditions, and control the flow of your program. In this article, we will explore the different comparison and logical operators available in Swift.

Comparison Operators

Comparison operators are used to compare values and determine their relationship. They return a boolean value of either true or false based on the comparison result. The grandparent of all comparison operators is the equal to. However, we use a single = for other purposes in Swift, so two are used to evaluate whether an object equals another. For example, to see if a is the same as b:

swift

```
if a == b {
    // Code to be executed if a is equal to b
}
```

The opposite of equality is inequality, which has its own operator to make code simpler to read. So use != to check for inequality. For example, to only process a given task if a and b are not equal:

swift

```
if a != b {
    // Code to be executed if a is not equal to b
}
```

Middle school taught us that the alligator eats the bigger number. This is still true in most programming languages, so there's no need to go back to middle school like Billy Madison had to. The greater than (>) is used in the following example as a standalone symbol (although we'll get more complicated in a bit) to evaluate that a variable called a is larger than the one called b:

swift

```
if a > b {
    // Code to be executed if a is greater than b
}
```

Or the less than remains consistent, so the following example will process the operation in the "if" if a is smaller than b:

swift

```
if a < b {
    // Code to be executed if a is less than b
}
```

It would suck if developers had to do an if to check for equality and then a greater than or less than sign to check if a variable is greater than or equal to another integer. Since before the advent of Euclidean geometry, we've also known that the greater than might also be greater than or equal to. We don't have closed and open circles on paper like we did in middle school; thus, we use the greater than or less than sign followed by the equal sign as our operator (>=). So to check if a is greater than or equal to b:

swift

```
if a >= b {
    // Code to be executed if a is greater than or equal to b
}
```

This same operator sequence works with less than or equal to (<=) as well:

swift

```
if a <= b {
    // Code to be executed if a is less than or equal to b
}
```

In the above examples, a and b are variables or values that are being compared. The comparison operators are used within if statements or other conditional constructs to evaluate conditions. However, developers can also apply much more complicated logic as well.

Logical Operators

Logical operators are used to combine conditions or to invert their results. They allow for complex conditions by combining simpler ones. This includes logic such as if two or more conditions are met, if one of two conditions are met, if multiple conditions are not met, and the merger of these into a more complicated bit of logic. We call these AND, OR, and NOT, respectively.

The logical AND is two ampersands (&&) in Swift, given that a single ampersand is reserved to indicate that a parameter is being passed as an inout variable. This is a common situation with operators, where what we might think of them as being from mathematics and real-life human grammar is a little different because the symbol itself is reserved for another task. But any time a double-ampersand is seen in Swift, just know that means a logical AND. It can be as simple as the following:

swift

```
if condition1 && condition2 {
    // Code to be executed if both condition1 and condition2 are true
}
```

The logical OR evaluates two different conditions and then runs if either one is true. The OR symbol is a pair of pipes (||), so the following stanza evaluates a pair of conditions and executes the code supplied if either is met:

swift

```
if condition1 || condition2 {
    // Code to be executed if either condition1 or condition2 is true
}
```

It is possible to write code that evaluates a statement and executes only if the statement is not correct by placing the condition in an else rather than an if; however, in many cases, it can be clearer to use a NOT instead - or execute a given if statement only if the value is not true. We refer to this as a logical NOT, and it can be as simple as placing an exclamation point in front of the condition, as follows:

swift

```
if !condition {
    // Code to be executed if the condition is false
}
```

To recap, as this is one of the most important pieces of logic to understand about any programming language: the logical AND operator (&&) returns true if both conditions are true. The logical OR operator (||) returns true if either of the conditions is true. The logical NOT operator (!) negates the result of the condition.

Combining Comparison and Logical Operators

Now let's start to make these operators more useful. It's fairly straightforward to combine comparison operators and logical operators to create vastly more complex conditions. We know that a can be greater than b and that c can be smaller than d, but what if we want both of those to be true? This is then written as follows:

swift

```
if a > b && c < d {
    // Code to be executed if the condition is true
}
```

Now let's extend the logic from the above example a bit further and look at what if both of those conditions are met OR if e is the same as f. Parentheses can be used to specify the order of evaluation, as seen in the second iteration with the added logic.

swift

```
if (a > b && c < d) || (e == f) {
    // Code to be executed if the condition is true
}
```

In the above code, the condition is true if either `(a > b && c < d)` or `(e == f)` is true. It's important to consider the precedence of operators when combining them. Parentheses can be used to override the default precedence and explicitly specify the order of evaluation.

Optional Chaining

The optional chaining operator (`?`) can safely access properties and methods of optional values. This allows for gracefully handling situations where the value might be nil. In the below example, the `passwordLength` variable is populated with a count of the characters in the password variable:

swift

```
let passwordLength = password?.count
```

In the above code, the `count` property of `password` is accessed only if `password` is not nil. If `password` had no value, this access would be skipped. This allows chaining together operations that are conditional on a value being present.

The use of optionals in Swift is probably the most confusing for anyone coming from Python or other scripted languages. Don't fear gentle reader! It takes some time to get the hang of optional and optional chaining, which we discuss next. Having said that, optionals are an incredibly powerful aspect of Swift that you will probably learn to love over time.

Model Classes When Optional Chaining

Optional chaining allows a developer to call properties, methods, and subscripts on an optional value and to check whether that value is nil before doing so. This makes code more concise and expressive code, especially when dealing with complex model classes.

Model classes are used to represent data. They can contain properties to store the data, and methods to work with the data. For example, the following code shows a simple model class to represent a person:

swift

```
class Password {
  var password: String?
  var age: Int?
  var length: Int?
  var specialCharacters: Int?
  func printPassword() {
    if let password = password {
      print("The password is \(password)!")
    } else {
      print("There is no password")
    }
  }
}
```

This model class has a number of properties: password, age, length, and special characters. All properties are optional, meaning that they can be nil. The `printPassword()` method checks whether the password property is nil. If it is nil, the method prints a notice that no password was set. Otherwise, it prints the password. But from here, provided that age, length, and whether it has special characters (by virtue of how many) are set, it could easily print more output indicating such.

Switch Statements and Pattern Matching

Developers commonly need to control the flow of data within programs based on multiple patterns. To continue with the password example, the rules an administrator sets to control allowed passwords might have more complicated logic. If a password doesn't meet a complexity requirement, such as having numbers or uppercase characters, or if the password is beyond a specified age, then it might be necessary to have an operation to send that password on to another part of a program and instead ask for another one.

One of the most common ways to deal with this would be with a switch statement.

Switch Statements

Switch statements are a powerful control flow construct in Swift that allow you to compare a value against multiple patterns and execute different code depending on the match. Switch statements are often used to handle different types of input or to select different code paths based on the current state of a program.

The syntax for a switch statement in Swift is as follows:

swift

```
switch value {
case pattern1:
  // Code to execute if pattern1 matches
case pattern2:
  // Code to execute if pattern2 matches
default:
  // Code to execute if no patterns match
}
```

The value in the switch statement is the value that will be compared against the patterns. The patterns are expressions that can be used to match the value. The case labels in the switch statement specify the patterns that will be matched. If a pattern matches the value, the code associated with the case label will be executed.

For example, the following switch statement will compare the value of the variable number against the patterns 1, 2, and 3:

swift

```
switch number {
case 1:
  print("The number is 1")
case 2:
```

```
  print("The number is 2")
case 3:
  print("The number is 3")
default:
  print("The number is not 1, 2, or 3")
}
```

If the value of number is 1, the code in the case 1: label will be executed. If the value of number is 2, the code in the case 2: label will be executed. And so on. If the value of number does not match any of the patterns, the code in the default: label will be executed.

Pattern Matching in Swift

Pattern matching is used to extract information about a value from its structure. Pattern matching can be used in a variety of contexts, including switch statements, for loops, and catch blocks. Some common patterns used in Swift (and other languages) include

- **Literal patterns**: Literal patterns match a specific literal value. For example, the pattern 1 matches the literal value 1.
- **Enumeration case patterns**: Enumeration case patterns match a case of an enumeration type. For example, the pattern .some matches the case `some` of the Optional enumeration.
- **Tuple patterns:** Tuple patterns match a tuple. For example, the pattern (1, "Hello, world!") matches the tuple (1, "Hello, world!").

When a pattern matches a value, the compiler extracts the information about the value that is specified by the pattern. This information can then be used in the code that is executed for the matching case. For example, the following switch statement uses pattern matching to extract the value of the variable `ipAddress`:

swift

```
switch ipAddress {
case .ipv4(let v4IPAddress):
  print("The IP address is v4 and is \(v4IPAddress)")
case .ipv6(let v6IPAddress):
```

```
  print("The IP address is v6 and is \(v6IPAddress)")
default:
  print("The IP address is neither v4 nor v6.")
}
```

Loops (For-In, While, and Repeat-While)

Loops are used to repeat a block of code a certain number of times. There are three types of loops in Swift: for-in loops, while loops, and repeat-while loops. Each are covered in the following sections.

For-In Loops

For-in loops are used to iterate over a collection of elements, such as an array, a range, or a string. The syntax for a for-in loop in Swift is as follows:

swift

```
for element in collection {
  // Code to execute for each element
}
```

The collection in the for-in loop is the collection of elements that you want to iterate over. The element in the for-in loop is a temporary variable that will be assigned each element in the collection, one at a time. The code inside the for-in loop will be executed for each element in the collection.

```
For example, the following code will print the elements of the array
numbers:
```

swift

```
let numbers = [1, 2, 3, 4, 5]
for number in numbers {
  print(number)
}
```

This code will print the following output:

swift

```
1
2
3
4
5
```

The for loop is useful when there's a known number of iterations or pattern to follow; however, the while loop is useful provided a boolean remains in a given state.

While Loops

While loops are used to repeat a block of code as long as a condition is true. The syntax for a while loop is as follows:

swift

```
while condition {
  // Code to execute while the condition is true
}
```

The condition in the while loop is a boolean expression that determines whether the loop should continue. The code inside the while loop will be executed as long as the condition is true. For example, the following code will print the numbers from 1 to 10:

swift

```
var i = 1
while i <= 10 {
  print(i)
  i += 1
}
```

This code will print the following output:

swift

```
1
2
3
```

```
4
5
6
7
8
9
10
```

The logic is simple, but given that more complex logic is often needed, it's also useful to have other types of while loops, like repeat-while.

Repeat-While Loops

Repeat-while loops are similar to while loops, but the code inside the loop is executed at least once, even if the condition is false. The syntax for a repeat-while loop is as follows:

swift

```
repeat {
  // Code to execute
} while condition
```

The condition in the repeat-while loop is a boolean expression that determines whether the loop should continue. The code inside the repeat-while loop will be executed once, and then the condition will be evaluated. If the condition is true, the code inside the loop will be executed again. This process will continue until the condition is false.

For example, the following code will print the numbers from 1 to 10:

swift

```
var i = 1
repeat {
  print(i)
  i += 1
} while i <= 10
```

This code will print the following output:

swift

```
1
2
3
4
5
6
7
8
9
10
```

There are also times when it's useful to, for whatever reason, break a loop at runtime. This is where control statements like break come into the arsenal of options Apple has provided in Swift. Given that there were expressions like BREAK in Konrad Zuse's Plankalkül (from the 1940s) and from a structured approach in CPL in the 1960s, BREAK has pretty much been a thing since the beginning of programming time. We just don't call it in caps any more – because we're not barbarians.

Control Flow Statements (Break and Continue)

Control flow statements are used to change the flow of execution of a program. They can be used to skip over code, to repeat code, or to exit from a loop or switch statement. There are two main control flow statements: break and continue. The break statement is used to exit from a loop or switch statement. When the break statement is executed, the program will immediately exit from the loop or switch statement, and the next line of code after the loop or switch statement will be executed.

The continue statement is used to skip to the next iteration of a loop. When the continue statement is executed, the program skips the rest of the code in the current iteration of the loop, and the next iteration of the loop is started.

The break and continue statements can be used together to create complex control flow structures. For example, the following code uses the break and continue statements to create a loop that only prints the even numbers from 1 to 10:

swift

```swift
for i in 1...10 {
    if i % 2 == 0 {
```

```
        print(i)
    } else {
        continue
    }
}
```

This code starts at the value of i = 1. Since i is not even, the continue statement is reached, and the loop skips to the next iteration. The code then continues to the next iteration of the loop. In the next iteration of the loop, the value of i is 2. Since i is even, the `print()` statement executes, and the value of i is printed. The code will then continue to the next iteration of the loop. This process will continue until the value of i reaches 10. At that point, the loop terminates and the program ends.

Use break to exit from a loop or switch statement when it is finished. Use continue to skip to the next iteration of a loop when it should execute apart from the rest of the code in the current iteration. Another way to accomplish similar tasks is with the guard keyword.

The Guard Keyword

The guard command is used to check a condition and, if the condition is not met, to execute some code and then exit the current scope. The guard command is often used to check for errors or to ensure that the correct values are passed to a function. The syntax for the guard command is the guard keyword followed by a condition and then an else, with the code to execute wrapped in curly brackets, as follows:

swift

```
guard <condition> else {
    // Code to execute if the condition is not met
}
```

To put this into a working example, the following code uses the guard command to check if a string called `userPassword` is not empty:

swift

```
func validate(userPassword: String) {
    guard !userPassword.isEmpty else {
        print("The string is empty.")
```

In the above example, the code is compiled only when using Swift 5.0 or later.

For runtime API availability checks, Swift uses conditions like `if #available(iOS 13, macOS 10.15, *)`.

The availability condition can conditionally compile code for different platforms as well as different versions of the operating system. For example, the following code will only be compiled if the running operating system is `iOS` or `macOS`:

swift

```
#if os(iOS) || os(macOS)
  print("This code will run on iOS or macOS.")
#endif
```

The availability condition can be used anywhere in code, but is most commonly used in conditional statements. This helps identify ways to intentionally cause compilation to fail. There are plenty of others – and ways to protect against them as well.

No Implicit Fallthrough

Switch statements do not have implicit fallthrough, which is different from other languages you may be used to. This means that a switch statement with multiple cases and no explicitly specified break statement will cause the control flow NOT to fall through to the next case. This is in contrast to C and Objective-C, where switch statements have implicit fallthrough. In C and Objective-C, a switch statement with multiple cases and no explicitly specified break statement, the control flow does actually fall through to the next case. The reason for the difference in behavior between Swift and C/Objective-C is that Swift is designed to be a more expressive language.

Here is an example of a switch statement in Swift:

swift

```
let value = 5
switch value {
case 1:
  print("The value is 1.")
case 2:
  print("The value is 2.")
case 3:
```

```
  print("The value is 3.")
default:
  print("The value is something else.")
}
```

In this example, the switch statement has four cases. If the value of value is 1, the case 1 clause will be executed. If the value of value is 2, the case 2 clause will be executed, and so on. If the value of value is not 1, 2, or 3, the default clause will be executed. Notice that there are no break statements in the switch statement.

To cause control flow to fall through to the next case, use the `fallthrough` statement. For example, the following code will print the values 1 and 2:

swift

```
let value = 1
switch value {
case 1:
  print("The value is 1.")
  fallthrough
case 2:
  print("The value is 2.")
default:
  print("The value is something else.")
}
```

In this example, the case 1 clause prints the value 1, and then the fallthrough statement causes the control flow to fall through to the case 2 clause. The case 2 clause then prints the value 2.

The lack of implicit fallthrough in Swift can be a bit jarring at first, if you are used to programming in C or Objective-C.

Interval Matching

Interval matching is a way to match a value against an interval. An interval is a range of values between two points. Interval matching can be used in switch statements, if statements, and guard statements. The following code shows an example of a switch statement that uses interval matching to match on the value of the number variable:

swift

```
let number = 10
switch number {
case 0..<10:
  print("The number is less than 10.")
case 10..<20:
  print("The number is between 10 and 20.")
case 20...:
  print("The number is greater than or equal to 20.")
default:
  print("The number is not valid.")
}
```

This code will print the following output to the console:

swift

```
The number is between 10 and 20.
```

The case statements use the ..< and ... operators to specify the intervals that they match. The ..< operator specifies an interval that excludes the upper bound, while the ... operator specifies an interval that includes the upper bound.

Tuples

Tuples are a way to group together multiple values of different types into a single value. Tuples can be used to represent a variety of things, such as

- A pair of coordinates
- A name and an age
- A product name and a price
- A date and time
- Creating tuples

To create a tuple, enclose the values in parentheses. The values can be of any type, and they can be separated by commas. For example, the following code creates a tuple with two values: a string and an integer:

swift

```
let person = ("Alice", 36)
```

Use the dot notation to access the values of a tuple. For example, the following code accesses the values of the above tuple:

swift

```
let name = person.0
let age = person.1
```

Tuples can also have more than two values. For example, the following code creates a tuple with three values: a string, an integer, and a double:

swift

```
let product = ("iPhone 13", 1000, 18.99)
```

Given that most information has multiple pieces of metadata to be tracked, understanding tuples is a key aspect of using variables in Swift. Another key concept is bindings.

Value Bindings

Value bindings bind matched values to constants or variables in a switch statement, using a case let statement. This can be useful for writing more concise and expressive code, especially when you need to match on multiple values or extract values from a complex structure. To use value bindings, use a case let statement in a switch statement.

The case let statement binds the matched value to the constant or variable that you specify. For example, the following code shows a switch statement that uses a value binding to match on the value of the number variable and bind the matched value to the constant `evenNumber`:

swift

```
let number = 10
switch number {
case let evenNumber where evenNumber % 2 == 0:
  print("The number is even: \(evenNumber).")
```

```
default:
  print("The number is odd.")
}
```

This code will print the following output to the console:

swift

```
The number is even: 10.
```

Use value bindings to extract values from a complex structure. For example, the following code shows a switch statement that uses a value binding to extract the x and y values from an (x, y) tuple:

swift

```
let (x, y) = (10, 20)
switch (x, y) {
case let (x, y) where x > y:
  print("The x value is greater than the y value: \(x), \(y).")
case let (x, y) where x < y:
  print("The x value is less than the y value: \(x), \(y).")
case let (x, y) where x == y:
  print("The x value is equal to the y value: \(x), \(y).")
default:
  print("The values are not valid.")
}
```

This code will print the following output to the console:

swift

```
The x value is less than the y value: 10, 20.
```

Another way to compose a more complex switch statement is with compound cases.

Compound Cases

A compound case is a single case in a switch statement that contains multiple values. These values are all checked against the switch statement's expression and are separated by commas. Compound cases can be used to make your code more concise and easier to read.

The following code shows an example of a switch statement with a compound case:

swift

```
let dayOfWeek = "Monday"
switch dayOfWeek {
case "Monday", "Tuesday", "Wednesday", "Thursday", "Friday":
  print("It's a weekday.")
case "Saturday", "Sunday":
  print("It's a weekend day.")
default:
  print("Invalid day of the week.")
}
```

This code will print the following output to the console:

swift

```
It's a weekday.
```

The compound case in this example matches on all of the weekdays. This means that we can use a single case to handle all of the weekdays, instead of having to write a separate case for each weekday.

Value-Binding Pattern

Value-binding patterns allow for binding the matched values to constants or variables in a switch statement, using a case let statement. This can be useful for writing more concise and expressive code, especially when matching based on multiple values or extracting values from a complex structure. The following code shows an example of a switch statement that uses a value-binding pattern to match on the value of the number variable:

swift

```
let number = 10
switch number {
case let evenNumber where evenNumber % 2 == 0:
  print("The number is even: \(evenNumber).")
case let oddNumber where oddNumber % 2 == 1:
```

```
  print("The number is odd: \(oddNumber).")
default:
  print("The number is not valid.")
}
```

This code will print the following output to the console:

swift

```
The number is even: 10.
```

The case let statement allows for binding the matched value to the constant `evenNumber` and use it in the body of the case. Use value-binding patterns to extract values from a complex structure. For example, the following code shows a switch statement that uses a value-binding pattern to extract the x and y values from an (x, y) tuple:

swift

```
let (x, y) = (10, 20)
switch (x, y) {
case let (x, y) where x > y:
  print("The x value is greater than the y value: \(x), \(y).")
case let (x, y) where x < y:
  print("The x value is less than the y value: \(x), \(y).")
case let (x, y) where x == y:
  print("The x value is equal to the y value: \(x), \(y).")
default:
  print("The values are not valid.")
}
```

This code prints the following output to the console:

swift

```
The x value is less than the y value: 10, 20.
```

The case let statement binds the matched values to the constants x and y and use them in the body of the case. It's also possible to match against values that may or may not exist.

Optional Patterns

Optional patterns are a way to match against optional values. They can be used to safely access the value of an optional or to handle the case where the optional value is nil.

Here's an example of how to extract the value, if one exists, from an optional integer:

swift

```
let number: Int? = 10
if let x = number {
  // The number is not nil.
  print(x) // Prints "10"
} else {
  // The number is nil.
  print("The number is nil.")
}
```

The if let statement is used to check if the optional pattern matched. If the pattern matched, the x variable will contain the value of the optional. If the pattern did not match, the else clause will be executed.

It's also possible to use optional patterns to match against multiple optional values. For example, the following code shows how to use an optional pattern to match against two optional integers:

swift

```
let number1: Int? = 10
let number2: Int? = 20
if let x = number1, let y = number2 {
  // Both number1 and number2 are not nil.
  print(x + y) // Prints "30"
} else {
  // At least one of number1 or number2 is nil.
  print("At least one of the numbers is nil.")
}
```

The if let statement will only be executed if both number1 and number2 are not nil. If either of the values is nil, the else clause will be executed.

Type-Casting Patterns

Type-casting patterns allow developers to write code that checks the type of an expression and casts it to another type if necessary. This is useful for writing more concise and expressive code. Type-casting patterns can be used in a variety of contexts, including

- Switch statements
- If statements
- Guard statements
- For-in loops

The following code shows an example of an if statement that uses a type-casting pattern to check the type of the value variable and cast it to an Int if possible:

swift

```
let value: Any = 10
if let intValue = value as? Int {
  print("The value is an integer: \(intValue).")
}
```

This code prints the following output to the console:

swift

```
The value is an integer: 10.
```

Type-casting helps prepare for other processes, like expression patterns.

Expression Patterns

Expression patterns allow for matching the value of an expression against a pattern and perform different actions depending on the match. Expression patterns can be used in a variety of contexts, such as with

- Switch statements
- If statements
- Guard statements
- For-in loops

The following code shows an example of an if statement that uses an expression pattern to match on the value of the number variable:

swift

```
let number = 10
if number == 10 {
  print("The number is 10.")
} else if number > 10 {
  print("The number is greater than 10.")
} else {
  print("The number is less than 10.")
}
```

This code will print the following output to the console:

swift

```
The number is 10.
```

Wildcard patterns can be used to match any value. For example, the following code shows an if statement that uses a wildcard pattern to match on any value:

swift

```
let number: Int? = 10
if let _ = number {
  print("The number is not nil.")
} else {
  print("The number is nil.")
}
```

This code will print the following output to the console:

swift

```
The number is not nil.
```

Tuple patterns can be used to match on multiple values. For example, the following code shows an if statement that uses a tuple pattern to match on the value of the (x, y) variable:

swift

```
let (x, y) = (10, 20)
if (x, y) == (10, 20) {
  print("The values are (10, 20).")
}
```

This code prints the following output to the console:

swift

```
The values are (10, 20).
```

Another pattern matching aspect is to take these expressions and review attached metadata, which we call attributes.

Attributes

Attributes are metadata that can be attached to types, declarations, and expressions. They provide additional information to the compiler, such as the intended use of a type or the meaning of a declaration. To use attributes, simply add the @ symbol followed by the attribute name to the type, declaration, or expression. For example, the following code shows how to use the `@objc` attribute to make a class compatible with Objective-C:

swift

```
@objc class MyClass {}
```

The following code shows how to use the `@available` attribute to make a function available only on certain platforms:

swift

```
@available(iOS 13.0, macOS 10.15, watchOS 6.0, *)
func myFunction() {}
```

You can also use attributes to define custom behavior for types, declarations, and expressions. For example, the following code shows how to use the `@propertyWrapper` attribute to define a custom property wrapper:

swift

```
@propertyWrapper
struct MyPropertyWrapper {
  var wrappedValue: Int
  init(wrappedValue: Int) {
    self.wrappedValue = wrappedValue
  }
}
```

This custom property wrapper can then be used to decorate properties in other classes, structs, and enums.

Attributes are a very large part of modern Swift and in particular SwiftUI. You'll see attributes used all over the place to reduce the complexity of the code. However, if you're starting out, the influx of attributes in the more complex parts of swfit, especially dealing with threading, may be overwhelming at first.

Conclusion

Control flow is what turns a list of statements into a program that makes decisions. The if-else statement, along with comparison and logical operators, handles most branching needs, while the switch statement and its pattern matching capabilities provide a more expressive way to handle multiple conditions, especially when combined with interval matching, tuples, value bindings, and compound cases. Loops handle repetition, with for-in for known collections and ranges, while and repeat-while for conditions evaluated at runtime, and break, continue, and labeled statements to fine-tune how those loops execute. The guard statement deserves special attention, as exiting early when requirements are not met keeps the happy path of a function unindented and readable, a pattern used throughout well-written Swift code.

Many of these constructs exist in some form in every programming language, but Swift adds its own conventions: switch statements that do not implicitly fall through, optionals that must be safely unwrapped before use, and availability conditions that keep code compatible across Apple's platforms. Developers coming from C, Objective-C, or a scripting language will find the concepts familiar even where the syntax differs, and the compiler is quick to point out the differences. Mastering these tools now pays off in every chapter that follows, since nearly all Swift code is built from these branches and loops.

The next chapter covers collections and arrays.

CHAPTER 4

Collections and Arrays

Arrays are fundamental data structures used to store and organize collections of related elements. An array is an ordered collection of elements, where each element has a unique index. Arrays can store values of any type, but all elements within a single array must be of the same type. You can create arrays to hold integers, strings, booleans, or even custom types.

Use square brackets [ ] following the element type to declare an array. Heres an example of declaring an array of integers:

swift

```
var numbers: [Int]
```

In the above code, the variable called `numbers` is declared, which holds an array of integers. The array hasn't been initialized yet, which is to say it hasn't been given a value yet (so it can't be used until it is).

Initialize and Access an Array

There are several ways to initialize an array with values. One common approach is to use an array literal, which allows a developer to specify the initial elements enclosed within square brackets [ ]. Let's make an example of three `IP` addresses, stored as strings:

swift

```
var IPs = ["10.0.0.1", "10.0.0.2", "10.0.0.3"]
```

In the code above, an array called `IPs` was declared and initialized with three strings. Individual elements can be obtained from an array using their index. Array indices start at 0. Here's an example, where the variable `firstIP` is populated with the object in the first entry of the array:

C. Edge et al., *Mastering Swift*, https://doi.org/10.1007/979-8-8688-2770-9_4

swift

```
let firstIP = IPs[0]  // Accessing the first element
print(firstIP)          // Output: "10.0.0.1"
```

Arrays stored in a var are mutable, which means their elements can be modified after creation. Assign new values to specific elements or use built-in methods to manipulate the array. Here's an example, where 10.0.0.3 is switched with 10.0.1.3:

swift

```
IPs[2] = "10.0.1.3"
print(IPs)
```

The output would then be as follows:

swift

```
["10.0.0.1", "10.0.0.2", "10.0.1.3"]
```

There are several operations to work with arrays. Here are a few commonly used ones:

1. `append(_:)`: Adds a new element to the end of the array
2. `insert(_:at:)`: Inserts an element at a specific index
3. `remove(at:)`: Removes the element at a given index
4. `count`: Returns the number of elements in the array
5. `isEmpty`: Checks if the array is empty
6. `contains(_:)`: Checks if the array contains a specific element

These provide built-in functionality to save time on iterating through arrays and manually editing them.

Iterating over an Array

One of the most common tasks developers will do with arrays is to iterate over the elements of an array using loops, such as `for-in`. This allows for operations on each element individually. Here's an example, picking up from the previous example of a list of IP addresses:

swift

```
for IP in IPs {
    print(IP)
}
```

The above code prints each IP in the IPs array on a new line, as follows:

swift

```
10.0.0.1
10.0.0.2
10.0.1.3
```

The simplest way to access an array element is through square bracket notation. Here's another example:

swift

```
let numbers = [1, 2, 3, 4, 5]
let thirdNumber = numbers[2]  // Accessing the element at index 2
print(thirdNumber)            // Output: 3
```

In the above code, the third element (index 2) of the numbers array is accessed with square brackets. Beyond that, there are also convenient properties to access the first and last elements of an array to make it simpler to access all objects.

swift

```
let vendors = ["Apple", "Microsoft", "Google"]
let firstVendor = vendors.first  // Accessing the first element
let lastVendor = vendors.last    // Accessing the last element
print(firstVendor)              // Output: Optional("Apple")
print(lastVendor)               // Output: Optional("Google")
```

Note that the first and last properties return optional values because an array could be empty. Of the other built-in methods to modify array elements, the following lines show how to use each:

swift

```
var numbers = [1, 2, 3, 4, 5]
numbers.append(6)              // Adding a new element at the end
```

```
numbers.insert(0, at: 0)        // Inserting an element at index 0
numbers.remove(at: 3)           // Removing the element at index 3
print(numbers)                  // Output: [0, 1, 2, 4, 5, 6]
```

The above code demonstrates adding an element to the end of the array using `append(_:)`, inserting an element at a specific index using `insert(_:at:)`, and removing an element at a given index using `remove(at:)`, which we'll cover in more detail in the next few sections.

Array Operations (Appending, Inserting, and Removing)

Appending elements to an array involves adding new elements at the end of the existing array. Swift provides a convenient method called `append(_:)` for this purpose. Let's explore how to append elements to an array:

swift

```
var vendors = ["Apple", "Microsoft"]
vendors.append("Google")        // Appending "Google" to the array
print(vendors)                  // Output: ["Apple", "Microsoft", "Google"]
```

In the above code, the `append(_:)` method was used to add the element "Google" to the `vendors` array. Inserting elements allows for adding new elements at a specific index within an array. Use the `insert(_:at:)` method for this operation, along with the position the element would appear in the resultant array. To use the numbers example from earlier, the following inserts the element 0 at index 0 of the `numbers` array using the `insert(_:at:)` method:

swift

```
var numbers = [1, 2, 3, 4]
numbers.insert(0, at: 0)        // Inserting 0 at index 0
print(numbers)                  // Output: [0, 1, 2, 3, 4]
```

Removing elements from an array is used to eliminate specific elements based on their index or value. There are multiple methods for removing elements, including `remove(at:)`, `removeLast()`, and `removeAll()`. The `remove(at:)` removes an element at a given index from the array. For example, the following removes the element at index 1 (Microsoft):

swift

```
var vendors = ["Apple", "Microsoft", "Google"]
vendors.remove(at: 1)          // Removing the element at index 1
print(vendors)                 // Output: ["Apple", "Google"]
```

The `removeLast()` removes the last element from the array. To remove the last element from the `numbers` array using the `removeLast()` method and capture its value, consider the following:

swift

```
var numbers = [1, 2, 3, 4]
let lastNumber = numbers.removeLast()  // Removing the last element and
capturing its value
print(numbers)                 // Output: [1, 2, 3]
print(lastNumber)              // Output: 4
```

The `removeAll()` removes all elements from the array, making it empty. The following uses the `removeAll()` method to remove all elements from the `vendors` array and then prints out the contents to confirm that it is now empty:

swift

```
var vendors = ["Apple", "Microsoft", "Google"]
vendors.removeAll()            // Removing all elements from the array
print(vendors.isEmpty)         // Output: true
```

These are useful for manipulating, but there are other options for looping, ordering, and filtering.

Working with Arrays: Iterating, Sorting, and Filtering

The methods to iterate over arrays, including `for-in` loops and higher-order functions like `forEach`, also reduce the amount of work required to complete basic work on arrays. The `for-in` loop is a common way to iterate over elements in an array. Here's an example:

swift

```
let numbers = [1, 2, 3, 4, 5]
for number in numbers {
    print(number)
}
```

The above iterates over each element in the numbers array and prints it on a new line. There's also a built-in method called forEach that allows developers to perform an operation on each element in a concise manner. As with the above options, this is accessed with a dot notation, following the name of the array. Here's an example:

swift

```
let vendors = ["Apple", "Microsoft", "Google"]
vendors.forEach { vendor in
    print(vendor)
}
```

In the above code, the forEach method iterates over each element in the vendors array and executes the provided closure for each element.

Sorting Array Elements

Sorting arrays rearranges elements in a specific order, such as ascending or descending. The sorted() method returns a new array with elements sorted in the desired order while keeping the original array unchanged. Here's an example:

swift

```
let numbers = [5, 3, 1, 4, 2]
let sortedNumbers = numbers.sorted()
print(sortedNumbers)  // Output: [1, 2, 3, 4, 5]
```

In the above code, the sorted() method sorts the numbers array in ascending order, producing a new array called sortedNumbers.

The sort() method sorts the elements of the array in-place, modifying the original array. Here's an example:

swift

```
var vendors = ["Apple", "Microsoft", "Google"]
vendors.sort()
print(vendors)  // Output: ["Apple", "Google", "Microsoft"]
```

In the above code, the `sort()` method sorts the `vendors` array in ascending order directly, and so Google appears before Microsoft.

Closure Expressions

Sorted is one form of a closure expression. Closure expressions, or simply closures as they're commonly referenced, are self-contained blocks of code that can be passed around and used in code-like functions. Closure expressions can be used to accomplish a few goals, including

- Passing them as arguments to functions and methods
- Returning them from functions and methods
- Storing them in variables and constants
- Using them as delegates and callbacks

To create a closure expression, simply put a function type inside curly braces. For example, the following code shows a closure expression that takes an integer as its argument and returns the double of that integer:

swift

```
let doubler: (Int) -> Int = { $0 * 2 }
```

This closure expression can be used in the same way as a regular function. For example, the following code shows how to call the closure expression to double the value of the number variable:

swift

```
let number = 10
let doubledNumber = doubler(number)
print(doubledNumber) // Prints 20
```

Closure expressions can also capture the context in which they are created. This means that closure expressions can access variables and constants that are defined outside of their closure body. For example, the following code shows a closure expression that captures the number variable:

swift

```
let number = 10
let adder: (Int) -> Int = { $0 + number }
print(adder(1)) // Prints 11
```

In this example, the adder closure expression captures the number variable and uses it to add 1 to the value that is passed to it.

Closures used to be a very popular way of allowing for asynchronous behavior in Swift; however, this has mostly been replaced with async/await in modern Swift.

Filtering Array Elements

Filtering array elements allows you to extract only the elements that meet specific conditions. The `filter()` method facilitates this process. For example:

swift

```
let numbers = [1, 2, 3, 4, 5]
let filteredNumbers = numbers.filter { number in
    number % 2 == 0
}
print(filteredNumbers)  // Output: [2, 4]
```

In the above code, the `filter()` method selects only the even numbers from the `numbers` array, creating a new array called `filteredNumbers`.

Iterating over an Array

Iterating over an array means accessing each element of the array one by one. This is a common task in programming, as it allows processing the elements of an array in a sequential manner. One of the most common ways to iterate over an array is a for loop over indices:

swift

```
let array = [1, 2, 3, 4, 5]
for i in 0..<array.count {
  // Do something with the element at index i
  print(array[i])
}
```

In this example, the for loop will iterate over the array variable, which is an array of integers. The i variable is used to keep track of the current index of the array. The loop will continue to iterate as long as the value of i is less than the number of elements in the array. The for-in loop is a common way to iterate over the elements directly. The syntax for a for-in loop is as follows:

swift

```
let array = [1, 2, 3, 4, 5]
for element in array {
  // Do something with the element
  print(element)
}
```

In this example, the for-in loop will iterate over the array variable, and each element of the array will be assigned to the element variable. The loop will continue to iterate as long as there are elements left in the array. The while loop can also be used to iterate over an array. The basic syntax for a while loop that iterates over an array is as follows:

swift

```
let array = [1, 2, 3, 4, 5]
var i = 0
while i < array.count {
  // Do something with the element at index i
  print(array[i])
  i += 1
}
```

In this example, the while loop will iterate over the array variable, and the i variable will be incremented after each iteration. The loop will continue to iterate as long as the value of i is less than the number of elements in the array.

The method you choose to iterate over an array will depend on your specific needs. Thus far, we've focused on integers and strings.

Creating an Array with an Array Literal

An array literal is a simple way of expressing a list of values in Swift. It is surrounded by square brackets, and the values in the array are separated by commas. For example, the following is an array literal that we've been using that contains the values 1, 2, 3, and 4:

swift

```
[1, 2, 3, 4]
```

To create an array with an array literal, simply surround a comma-separated list of values with square brackets. The type of the array will be inferred from the values in the array literal. For example, the numbers array we've used throughout this chapter creates an array of integers:

swift

```
let numbers = [1, 2, 3, 4]
```

The numbers variable is an array of integers because the array literal contains only integers, and integer literals default to `Int` unless the context specifies a different type. In addition to using an array literal, the following initializers can be used:

- `init()`: Creates a new, empty array
- `init(repeating:count:)`: Creates a new array that contains the specified number of a single, repeated value
- `init(_ elements: [Element])`: Creates a new array that contains the elements of the specified array

An array literal is a simple and convenient way to create an array in Swift. You can use an array literal to create an array of any type, and the type of the array will be inferred from the values in the array literal.

To create an array of strings, simply quote the contents of the array, as follows, which defines an array called `stringsArray`:

swift

```
let stringsArray = ["Hello", "World"]
```

To create an array of floating point numbers, simply include the dot that indicates it's a float:

swift

```
let numbersArray = [1.0, 2.0, 3.0, 4.0]
```

To create an array of booleans, simply include only true or false in the array.

swift

```
let booleanArray = [true, false, true, false]
```

Attempting to mix and match elements of different types could cause an error that "heterogeneous collection literal could only be inferred to '[Any]'; add explicit type annotation if this is intentional" - which roughly means that the array needs to be set to hold anything when created, which can include multidimensional arrays.

Multidimensional Arrays and Nested Loops

Arrays can contain elements of any type, including other arrays. These nested arrays create what are known as multidimensional arrays, typically used to organize data in a structured and hierarchical manner. A multidimensional array is an array of arrays, forming a grid-like structure with multiple dimensions.

Each element within a multidimensional array represents a value at a specific position. For example, a 2D array can be visualized as a table with rows and columns, while a 3D array resembles a cube with layers.

Declaring and Initializing Multidimensional Arrays

To declare a multidimensional array in Swift, you can use the syntax `[[Element]]`, where `Element` represents the type of the array's elements. Here's an example of declaring and initializing a 2D array:

swift

```
var grid: [[Int]] = [[1, 2, 3], [4, 5, 6], [7, 8, 9]]
```

The above code declares a 2D array called `grid` that holds integers. The initialization specifies the elements using nested arrays, creating a grid-like structure.

Accessing Elements in Multidimensional Arrays

To access elements within a multidimensional array, you need to specify the indices for each dimension. This requires using multiple sets of square brackets. Here's an example:

swift

```
let element = grid[1][2]
print(element)  // Output: 6
```

The above code is used to access the element at row 1, column 2 within the `grid` array.

Nested Loops for Multidimensional Arrays

Nested loops play a crucial role in working with multidimensional arrays. They allow you to traverse through each dimension of the array, accessing and manipulating individual elements effectively. Let's see an example of using nested loops to iterate over a 2D array:

swift

```
let grid = [[1, 2, 3], [4, 5, 6], [7, 8, 9]]
for row in grid {
    for element in row {
        print(element)
    }
}
```

The above code uses two nested loops. The outer loop iterates over each row in the `grid` array, while the inner loop iterates over each element within the row. This is used to access and perform operations on each element individually.

Manipulating Multidimensional Arrays

Nested loops allow developers to perform various operations on multidimensional arrays, such as modifying elements or applying algorithms across the entire array. Here's an example of updating elements within a 2D array using nested loops:

swift

```
var grid = [[1, 2, 3], [4, 5, 6], [7, 8, 9]]
```

```
for i in 0..<grid.count {
    for j in 0..<grid[i].count {
        grid[i][j] *= 2
    }
}
print(grid)
```

The above code is used on nested loops to iterate over each element in the `grid` array and multiply each by 2. This modifies the original array, resulting in every element being doubled. Then it's possible to effectively navigate through the dimensions of multidimensional arrays and access or modify individual elements. This is useful when working with tables, matrices, or other complex datasets; multidimensional arrays and nested loops help to get various bits of information into a form where they can be easily processed. Not all data is so simple and some needs to be more persistent; so, in the next chapter, we'll dig further into other ways to handle these operations, like dictionaries and sets.

Conclusion

Arrays are the workhorse collection type in Swift: an ordered list of elements of a single type, accessed by index, and backed by a rich set of built-in methods. Between array literals for creation, `append(_:)`, `insert(_:at:)`, and the various remove methods for manipulation, and properties like `count`, `first`, and `last` for inspection, most everyday array work never requires writing a loop by hand. When iteration is needed, there are several options - for-in loops, index-based loops, while loops, and `forEach` - and higher-order functions like `sorted()` and `filter()` take a closure to express what to do with each element rather than how to walk the collection. Closures come up again and again in Swift, so if you need more discussion of them, we do that later in the book.

A few details are easy to trip over at first: indices start at 0, accessing an index that does not exist crashes at runtime, and `first` and `last` return optionals because an array might be empty. Arrays declared with `let` are immutable while those declared with `var` can change, and every element must share a type unless the array is explicitly declared to hold `Any`. For grid-like or hierarchical data, arrays can be nested into multidimensional arrays and traversed with nested loops. Ordered collections are not the right shape for every problem, though sometimes data needs to be looked up by a key rather than a position or duplicates need to be impossible by design.

The next chapter covers dictionaries and sets.

CHAPTER 5

Dictionaries and Sets

Dictionaries and sets are two of the most commonly used collection types. They are both unordered collections, but have different strengths and weaknesses. Dictionaries are used to store key-value pairs. The keys are unique identifiers, and the values can be of any type. Dictionaries are a good choice when you need to be able to look up values by their keys. For example, you might use a dictionary to store a mapping of names to addresses.

Sets are used to store unique values. The order of the elements in a set does not matter. Sets are a good choice when you need to be able to quickly determine whether a value is present in the collection. For example, you might use a set to store a list of all the words in a dictionary.

Table 5-1 summarizes the key differences between dictionaries and sets.

Table 5-1. *Dictionaries vs. Sets*

Feature	Dictionary	Set
Order	Unordered	Unordered
Uniqueness	Values can be duplicated	Values must be unique
Lookup	By key	By value
Membership	Fast	Very fast

Here are some examples of when you might use dictionaries:

- Storing a mapping of names to addresses
- Storing a mapping of product IDs to product names
- Storing a mapping of user IDs to user preferences

C. Edge et al., *Mastering Swift*, https://doi.org/10.1007/979-8-8688-2770-9_5

And it might be better to use sets when

- Storing a list of all the words in a dictionary
- Storing a list of all the unique users who have visited a website
- Storing a list of all the possible moves in a game

Understanding Dictionaries and Their Syntax

Dictionaries are fundamental data structures that are used to store and retrieve key-value pairs. Unlike arrays, which use integer indices, dictionaries provide a way to associate values with unique keys. A dictionary is an unordered collection of key-value pairs, where each key is unique within the dictionary. Keys are used to access and retrieve corresponding values. Dictionaries are commonly used when storing and retrieving data based on specific identifiers or labels.

To declare a dictionary, use the syntax `[Key: Value]`, where `Key` represents the type of the keys, and `Value` represents the type of the associated values. Here's an example of declaring and initializing a dictionary:

swift

```
var devices: [String: Int] = ["iPhone": 356, "MacBook": 285, "Watch": 495]
```

In the above code, we declared a dictionary called `devices` with keys of type `String` and values of type `Int`.

Accessing and Modifying Dictionary Values

To access values in a dictionary, use the associated key. This allows for retrieving the corresponding value. Additionally, modify existing values or add new key-value pairs as needed. Let's see some examples:

swift

```
var devices: [String: Int] = ["iPhone": 356, "MacBook": 285, "Watch": 495]
```

To then access a key, let's create a new variable for the user's iPhone:

swift

```
let useriPhone = devices["iPhone"]
print(useriPhone)
```

Let's say the MacBook ID changed from 285 to 654. To modify the value for the key MacBook:

swift

```
devices["MacBook"] = 654
```

To add a new device, let's say called Vision with an ID key of 792:

swift

```
devices["Vision"] = 792
print(devices)
```

In the above code, the value for the key "Vision" is set using square bracket notation. These examples cover how to access and manipulate data in specific keys, but it's also possible to iterate through all items in the collection.

Iterating over Dictionary Elements

To traverse through the key-value pairs of a dictionary, Swift provides several ways, including `for-in` loops, the `keys` and `values` properties, and the `forEach` method. Let's explore these options:

swift

```
var devices: [String: Int] = ["iPhone": 356, "MacBook": 285, "Watch": 495]
for (name, deviceID) in devices {
    print("\(name): \(deviceID)")
}
for name in devices.keys {
    print(name)
}
for deviceID in devices.values {
    print(deviceID)
}
devices.forEach { (name, deviceID) in
    print("\(name): \(deviceID)")
}
```

The above code demonstrates different approaches to iterate over the dictionary's key-value pairs, keys, and values. Each iteration provides access to the corresponding key and value, allowing you to perform operations based on the data.

Adding, Accessing, and Modifying Dictionary Entries

Dictionaries provide a convenient way to associate values with unique keys, allowing for efficient retrieval and modification of data. To add new entries to a dictionary, assign a value to a specific key. To add entries, use the brackets, with each key-value pair included. For example, to create a collection of volumes with free space:

swift

```
var volumes: [String: String] = ["Macintosh HD": "30", "Backup HD": "10"]
volumes["Recovery"] = "88"
volumes["External HD"] = "20"
```

In the above code, we have a dictionary called `volumes` with initial key-value pairs. To add new entries, we simply assign a value to a new key, such as "Recovery" and "External HD". The dictionary will now contain these additional entries.

Accessing Dictionary Entries

Accessing dictionary entries involves retrieving values based on their associated keys. Swift provides several methods to access dictionary entries, including subscript syntax and optional binding. Let's explore these options:

swift

```
var volumes: [String: String] = ["Macintosh HD": "30", "Backup HD": "10"]
let macintoshFreeSpace = volumes["Macintosh HD"]
if let backupFreeSpace = volumes["Backup HD"] {
    print(backupFreeSpace)
}
```

In the above code, we accessed the values for the keys "Macintosh HD" and "Backup HD" using the subscript syntax. The value for the key "Macintosh HD" is assigned to `macintoshFreeSpace`, while the value for the key "Backup HD" is assigned to `backupFreeSpace` within the optional binding. We can safely unwrap the optional value and print it.

Modifying Dictionary Entries

Modifying dictionary entries involves changing the value associated with a specific key. Swift allows for direct modification by assigning a new value to an existing key. Let's see an example:

swift

```
var volumes: [String: String] = ["Macintosh HD": "30", "Backup HD": "10"]
volumes["Macintosh HD"] = "20"
```

In the above code, we modified the value for the key "Macintosh HD" by assigning it a new value of "20". The dictionary entry for "Macintosh HD" now reflects the updated value.

Removing Dictionary Entries

To remove entries from a dictionary, you use the `removeValue(forKey:)` method or assign `nil` to the key. Let's see an example:

swift

```
var volumes: [String: String] = ["Macintosh HD": "30", "Backup HD": "10"]
volumes.removeValue(forKey: "Macintosh HD")
volumes["Backup HD"] = nil
```

In the above code, the entry for the key "Macintosh HD" is removed using the `removeValue(forKey:)` method. The entry for the key "Backup HD" is assigned `nil` after that. After removing the entries, the dictionary no longer `contains` these key-value pairs.

Everything is there to now seamlessly add new entries, retrieve values based on keys, and modify existing entries in dictionaries. As the collection grows, iteration and filtering become more difficult.

Iterating and Filtering Dictionary Entries

Iterating over dictionary entries and filtering them based on specific conditions allows you to perform operations selectively. Swift provides various techniques, including `for-in` loops, the `keys` and `values` properties, and the `filter(_:)` method. Let's explore an example:

swift

```
let volumes = ["Macintosh HD": 30, "Backup HD": 10, "Recovery": 88]
for (name, freeSpace) in volumes {
    print("\(name) has \(freeSpace) free space")
}
let enoughSpace = volumes.filter { $0.value >= 70 }
print(enoughSpace)
```

In the above code, we iterate over the dictionary entries using a `for-in` loop. Additionally, we use the `filter(_:)` method to create a new dictionary containing only the entries where the free space is greater than or equal to 70.

Merging dictionaries allows for consolidating or updating data from multiple sources. Removing entries eliminates specific key-value pairs based on keys, facilitating data management. Furthermore, iterating and filtering dictionary entries provides flexibility in performing selective operations.

Sets and Their Unique Element Property

A set is an unordered collection of unique elements. It does not rely on indices like arrays, and the order of elements is not guaranteed. Sets are particularly useful when you need to work with data where uniqueness matters more than the order. By ensuring that each element in a set is unique, sets allow for efficient membership tests and operations. Unlike arrays or dictionaries, sets do not allow duplicate values, making them useful when dealing with collections that require distinct elements.

Sets and Hash Types

Sets are collections of unique values. This means that no two elements in a set can have the same value. Sets are implemented using hashing, which stores elements based on a hash value derived from each element. The hash value is used to determine where the element is stored internally.

If two elements have the same hash value, this is a hash collision. Hash collisions can occur because the hash function is not perfect. However, the hash function is designed to minimize the number of hash collisions. When you remove an element from a set, the set's hash function is used to calculate the element's hash value. The hash value is then used to find the location of the element in the hash table. The element is then removed from the hash table. Hash values are an important part of set types. They allow sets to store unique values and to quickly find elements in the set.

The hash function for a set type is a function that takes an element as input and returns a hash value. Hash collisions are handled internally by the set implementation.

Declaration and Initialization of Sets

Declare and initialize sets with the `Set` type. Sets can hold elements of any hashable type, which includes most of the fundamental built-in types in the Swift language, like integers, strings, and even custom types that conform to the `Hashable` protocol. Here's an example of declaring and initializing sets:

swift

```
var deviceTypes: Set<String> = ["iPhone", "iPad", "MacBook", "Watch",
"iBook"]
var numbers: Set<Int> = [1, 2, 3, 4, 5]
```

In the above code, we declared two sets: `deviceTypes` and `numbers`. The first set holds string elements, while the second set holds integer elements. The sets are initialized with a list of values using an array literal syntax.

Adding and Removing Elements from a Set

Sets in Swift provide convenient methods for adding and removing elements. The `insert(_:)` method allows you to add a new element to a set, while the `remove(_:)` method enables you to remove an element. Let's see an example:

swift

```
var deviceTypes: Set<String> = ["iPhone", "iPad", "iBook", "iMac",
"MacBook", "Watch"]
deviceTypes.insert("Vision")
deviceTypes.remove("iBook")
```

The above code is used to add the element "Vision" to the `deviceTypes` set using the `insert(_:)` method. The element "iBook" is then removed from the set using the `remove(_:)` method, since most of those are probably retired by now (having not been made since 2006). After these operations, the set `deviceTypes` no longer `contains` "iBook" but now includes Jeremy Bannister, Joel Rennich, Charles Edge. "Vision". Turns out that the number of `deviceTypes` in Apple's lineup doesn't change that often, but the names do change every now and then.

Set Membership

To check if an element is a member of a set, you can use the `contains()` method. The `contains()` method takes an element as input and returns a boolean value indicating whether or not the element is a member of the set.

For example, the following code checks if the number 5 is a member of the set `mySet`:

swift

```
let mySet = Set([1, 2, 3, 4, 6])
if mySet.contains(5) {
  print("5 is a member of the set.")
} else {
  print("5 is not a member of the set.")
}
```

To check if two sets are equal, use the == operator. The == operator returns a boolean value indicating whether or not the two sets have the same elements. For example, the following code checks if the set `mySet` is equal to the set `yourSet`:

swift

```
let mySet = Set([1, 2, 3, 4, 6])
let yourSet = Set([1, 2, 3, 4, 6])
if mySet == yourSet {
  print("The sets are equal.")
} else {
  print("The sets are not equal.")
}
```

In addition to checking if a value is present in a collection, this if/then manner of checking membership can also be used to `filter` a collection based on its membership in another collection and to compare two collections to see if they contain the same elements.

Performing Set Operations

Sets support various operations to manipulate and compare sets. Some commonly used operations include union, intersection, and subtraction. To perform a union, it's possible to create a new set, which in the below code is simply called union. Notice that dot notation is used to call `setA.union(setB)`.

Let's explore these operations using examples:

swift

```
let setA: Set<Int> = [1, 2, 3, 4, 5]
let setB: Set<Int> = [4, 5, 6, 7, 8]
let union = setA.union(setB)
print(union)
```

When you print a set, you'll see all the elements (order is not guaranteed):

swift

```
[1, 2, 3, 4, 5, 6, 7, 8]
```

The intersection is used to identify similarities between the two sets, where the same syntax as the union is followed - but using intersection as the keyword.

swift

```
let setA: Set<Int> = [1, 2, 3, 4, 5]
let setB: Set<Int> = [4, 5, 6, 7, 8]
let intersection = setA.intersection(setB)
print(intersection)
```

The output identifies the items that intersected (order is not guaranteed):

swift

```
[4, 5]
```

Subtraction does the same, where the elements of `setB` are removed from `setA`.

swift

```
let setA: Set<Int> = [1, 2, 3, 4, 5]
let setB: Set<Int> = [4, 5, 6, 7, 8]
let difference = setA.subtracting(setB)
print(difference)
```

The output `contains` the elements that remain in `setA` (order is not guaranteed): *swift*

```
[1, 2, 3]
```

The unique element property of sets ensures that each element appears only once. If attempting to add a duplicate element to a set, it will be ignored.

Conclusion

Dictionaries and sets round out Swift's core collection types, and choosing between them - or an array - comes down to how the data will be accessed. When values need to be looked up by a meaningful key rather than a position, a dictionary is the right shape: subscript syntax handles adding, reading, and updating entries, `removeValue(forKey:)` or assigning nil removes them, and the same iteration and filtering tools that work on arrays work on key-value pairs. When what matters is uniqueness and fast membership tests, a set is the answer, with `insert(_:)`, `remove(_:)`, and `contains()` covering the basics and operations like union, intersection, and subtraction handling comparisons between whole collections at once.

Two details from this chapter are worth carrying forward. First, both collections are unordered - code should never depend on the sequence in which a dictionary's or set's elements appear, which is why the printed output in the examples can vary from run to run. Second, dictionary subscript access returns an optional, because the key might not be present; unwrapping those values safely with optional binding is the same pattern used with an array's `first` and `last`, and it becomes second nature quickly. Under the hood, both types rely on hashing, which is what makes lookups and membership tests so fast and why set and dictionary key types must be hashable.

The next chapter covers functions and closures.

CHAPTER 6

Functions and Closures

Functions and closures are both blocks of code that can be reused, but they have different strengths and weaknesses. Functions are named blocks of code that can be invoked from anywhere in your program. They help to encapsulate a piece of functionality and to make it reusable, for example, to define a function to calculate the factorial of a number or any other mathematical operation or to format a string.

Closures are anonymous blocks of code that can be passed around and used as values. They are a good choice when passing a piece of functionality to another function or method. For example, use a `closure` to specify the action that should be taken when a button is clicked. They're also used to filter a collection of data or implement callback functions.

In general, use functions to encapsulate a piece of functionality and make it reusable. Use closures to pass a piece of functionality to another function or method. Consider the information in Table 6-1 when choosing when to use each.

Table 6-1. *Functions vs. Closures*

Feature	Function	Closure
Name	Has a name	Does not have a name
Scope	Global or local	Local
Reusability	Reused from anywhere	Can be reused only in defined scope
Passing as arguments	Can be passed as arguments to other functions	Can be passed as arguments to other functions
Capturing values	Can capture values from its surrounding context	Can capture values from its surrounding context

C. Edge et al., *Mastering Swift*, https://doi.org/10.1007/979-8-8688-2770-9_6

Initialization is the process of preparing an instance of a class, structure, or enumeration for use. Deinitialization is the process of cleaning up after an instance of a class, structure, or enumeration is no longer needed.

Initialization

Initialization is typically done with initializers. Initializers are special methods used to create new instances of a class, structure, or enumeration. Initializers can take parameters, which can be used to specify the initial values of the instance's properties. In classes, there are designated initializers and convenience initializers.

Designated initializers are the primary initializers for a class. They must initialize all of the instance's stored properties. Convenience initializers are optional initializers that can be used to create new instances of a class with a subset of the instance's stored properties.

Deinitialization

Deinitialization is done with deinitializers. Deinitializers are special methods that are called when an instance of a class is no longer needed. Deinitializers can be used to clean up after the instance, such as releasing resources or closing files. A deinitializer takes no parameters and returns no value. The following code shows an example of a class with an initializer and a deinitializer:

swift

```
class Person {
  var name: String
  var loginAttempts: Int
  init(name: String, loginAttempts: Int) {
    self.name = name
    self.loginAttempts = loginAttempts
  }
  deinit {
    print("Person \(name) has been deinitialized.")
  }
}
```

To create a new instance of the Person class, we can use the initializer:

swift

```
let person = Person(name: "Charles", loginAttempts: 6)
```

When the instance is no longer referenced, the deinitializer will be called to clean up after it.

Arguments

An argument is a value that is passed to a function when it is called. The function uses the arguments to perform its task. For example, the following function takes two arguments, a and b, and returns their sum:

swift

```
func sum(a: Int, b: Int) -> Int {
  return a + b
}
```

To call this function, pass two values, such as 2 and 3, as arguments:

swift

```
let sum = sum(a: 2, b: 3)
```

The value of sum would then be 5, which is the sum of 2 and 3.

Argument Labels

In Swift, arguments can have argument labels. Argument labels are used to identify the arguments when calling a function.

For example, the following function has two arguments, with argument labels "first" and "second":

swift

```
func sum(first a: Int, second b: Int) -> Int {
  return a + b
}
```

To call this function, we would pass two values, such as 2 and 3, as arguments, and we would use the argument labels to identify them:

swift

```
let sum = sum(first: 2, second: 3)
```

Argument labels are optional, but they can make your code more readable.

Generic Argument Clause

Generic argument clauses are a way to specify additional requirements on the type parameters of a generic function or type. To use a generic argument clause, add a where clause to the function or type declaration. The where clause can contain any number of requirements on the type parameters. For example, the following code shows a generic function that takes two values of any type and returns the sum of those values, but only if the types conform to the `Numeric` protocol (e.g., standard number types such as `Int` and `Double`):

swift

```
func add<T>(a: T, b: T) -> T where T: Numeric {
  return a + b
}
```

If the `add()` function is called with a type that does not conform to the `Numeric` protocol, the compiler will generate an error. Generic argument clauses can also be used to constrain associated types. For example, the following code shows a simplified "sequence-like" protocol that defines a `map()` method that takes a `closure` as an argument and returns a new collection with the results of applying the `closure` to each element of the original collection:

swift

```
protocol SimpleSequence {
  associatedtype Element
  func forEach(_ body: (Element) -> Void)
  func map<T>(transform: (Element) -> T) -> [T]
}
```

The `map()` method can be implemented for any type that conforms to the `SimpleSequence` protocol. The following code shows a generic implementation of the `map()` method:

swift

```
extension SimpleSequence {
  func map<T>(transform: (Element) -> T) -> [T] {
    var result = [T]()
    forEach { element in
      result.append(transform(element))
    }
    return result
  }
}
```

For example, the following code shows how to use the `map()` method to double all the elements in an array of integers:

swift

```
let numbers: [Int] = [1, 2, 3, 4, 5]
```

It's then possible to double all the elements in the array using the `map()` method and print the doubled array:

swift

```
let doubledNumbers = numbers.map { $0 * 2 }
print(doubledNumbers)
```

This will print the following output to the console:

swift

```
[2, 4, 6, 8, 10]
```

Doubling numbers is a simple operation, but we could have done far more complicated tasks. As the code becomes more complex, we want to keep more of it reusable – and so it's time to cover functions.

Declare and Use Functions

A function is a sequence of code, or instructions, that performs a specific task. This code is packaged as a unit that can be called in other areas of code. Functions are used to encapsulate reusable blocks of code, promote modularity, and enhance the organization of code.

Functions are declared using the `func` keyword, followed by the function name, parameters, return type, and the body of the function enclosed in curly braces. Let's look at a simple example:

swift

```
func greet(name: String) {
    print("Hello, \(name)!")
}
```

In the above code, a function named `greet` is declared that takes a parameter `name` of type `String`. The function body prints a greeting message using the provided name.

Calling Functions

Once a function is declared, it is called by its name, followed by parentheses. If the function has parameters, the arguments go in the parentheses. Let's call the `greet` function from the previous example:

swift

```
greet(name: "Charles")
```

In the above code, the `greet` function passes the argument "Charles" for the `name` parameter. As a result, the function prints "Hello, Charles!" to the console.

Function Parameters and Return Values

Functions can have parameters and return values, which allow data to be passed into the function and results, or values, to be received back. Let's see an example of a function with parameters and a return value:

swift

```
func addNumbers(_ a: Int, _ b: Int) -> Int {
    return a + b
}
```

The above code is used to declare a function named addNumbers that takes two parameters a and b, both of type Int. The function adds a and b together and returns the result as an Int. The addNumbers function is then called and the return value(s) used like this:

swift

```
let sum = addNumbers(5, 3)
print("The sum is: \(sum)") // Output: The sum is: 8
```

In the above code, the addNumbers function received arguments 5 and 3. The return value, 8, is stored in the sum variable and printed to the console.

Function Overloading

It's also possible to declare multiple functions with the same name but different parameters, known as function overloading. This allows you to create functions that perform similar tasks but with different input types or numbers of parameters. Let's see an example:

swift

```
func square(_ number: Int) -> Int {
    return number * number
}
func square(_ number: Double) -> Double {
    return number * number
}
```

The above code was used to declare two square functions, one that takes an Int parameter and another that takes a Double parameter. Both functions calculate the square of the given number but work with different types. So far, the function has used a single type.

Generic Functions

Generic functions are functions that can be used with different types of data. This is achieved by using type parameters, which are placeholders for the types that will be used when the function is called. For example, the following code shows a generic function that takes two values of any type and returns the sum of those values:

swift

```
func add<T>(a: T, b: T) -> T where T: Numeric {
  return a + b
}
```

This function can be called with any types that conform to the `Numeric` protocol, such as `Int`, Float, and `Double`. For example, the following code shows how to call the `add()` function with two integers:

swift

```
let sum = add(a: 1, b: 2)
```

The sum variable will now contain the value 3. Another example of a generic function is the `map()` function. The `map()` function takes a `closure` as an argument and returns a new collection with the results of applying the `closure` to each element of the original collection. The following code shows a generic implementation of the `map()` function:

swift

```
func map<T, U>(array: [T], transform: (T) -> U) -> [U] {
  var result = [U]()
  for element in array {
    result.append(transform(element))
  }
  return result
}
```

This function can be called with any array, and the return type is inferred from the transform `closure`.

Function Parameters and Return Types

Function parameters and return types are used to pass data into functions and receive results back, which helps to reduce cyclomatic complexity and so the modularity in code. Function parameters are the variables or constants used to pass data into a function. They define the input values that the function expects to perform its task. Parameters can have names, types, and additional attributes that control their behavior. Let's examine the different aspects of function parameters:

Provide names for each parameter when declaring functions. The parameter names are used when calling the function to indicate the corresponding values being passed. The previous example of the greet function had a single parameter with no default values. However, parameters can have default values as well. If a default value is provided, callers can omit that argument. The following example builds on the greet function, but adds the default name of Guest:

swift

```
func greet(name: String = "Guest") {
    print("Hello, \(name)!")
}
```

When calling the function without providing an argument, the default value "Guest" is used. However, when passing an argument, such as any name, it overrides the default value.

Function Return Types

The return type of a function determines the type of value it returns when the function is called. Functions can return a wide range of data types, including fundamental types, custom types, or even tuples. Let's explore the concept of function return types: to declare the return type of a function, you specify the type immediately after the closing parenthesis of the parameter list, using the arrow (->) notation. Here's an example:

swift

```
func addNumbers(a: Int, b: Int) -> Int {
    return a + b
}
let sum = addNumbers(a: 5, b: 3)
print("The sum is: \(sum)") // Output: The sum is: 8
```

```
  return value * 2
}) // doubledArray is equal to [2, 4, 6]
```

It's also fairly straightforward to take a type and declare an alias for it.

Type Alias Declarations

Type alias declarations are used to create a new name for an existing type. To declare a type alias, use the typealias keyword followed by the name of the type alias and the type that you want to alias. For example, the following code declares a type alias for the `String` type:

swift

```
typealias MyString = String
```

Once a type alias is declared, use it anywhere that the original type would otherwise be used. The following shows how to use the `MyString` type alias to declare a variable:

swift

```
let myString: MyString = "Hello, world!"
```

You can also use type aliases to declare generic types. For example, the following code shows how to declare a type alias for a generic dictionary type:

swift

```
typealias MyDictionary<Key, Value> = [Key: Value]
```

This type alias can then be used to declare a dictionary variable, as shown in the following code:

swift

```
let myDictionary: MyDictionary<String, Int> = ["one": 1, "two": 2,
"three": 3]
```

Managing the number of arguments for functions and methods can become daunting as code grows – thus variadic parameters.

Variadic Parameters

Variadic parameters are functions or methods that can accept a variable number of arguments. They are useful for functions that need to work with a variety of input data, such as functions that print to the console or functions that perform mathematical operations on a list of numbers. To declare a variadic parameter, you use the ... (ellipsis) character after the type of the parameter. For example, the following code shows a function that accepts a variable number of integer arguments:

swift

```
func sum(numbers: Int...) -> Int {
  var total = 0
  for number in numbers {
    total += number
  }
  return total
}
```

The numbers parameter in the above function is a variadic parameter. This means that the function can be called with any number of integer arguments. For example, the following code shows how to call the `sum()` function with one, two, and three integer arguments:

swift

```
let sum1 = sum(numbers: 1) // sum1 is equal to 1
let sum2 = sum(numbers: 1, 2) // sum2 is equal to 3
let sum3 = sum(numbers: 1, 2, 3) // sum3 is equal to 6
```

Variadic parameters can be used in both functions and methods. They are also supported in generic functions and methods. Another type of argument to be covered is in-out parameters.

In-Out Parameters

An in-out argument is a variable that can be modified by the function that it is passed to. To declare an in-out argument, you use the & symbol before the variable name. For example, the following function takes an in-out argument, number, and increments its value by 1:

Inheritance is the principle that allows objects to inherit properties and behaviors from a superclass or base class. It establishes a hierarchical relationship between classes, where subclasses can inherit and extend the characteristics of their parent class. Inheritance promotes code reuse, as subclasses can inherit and override methods and properties, adding specialized behavior while maintaining common functionality.

Polymorphism is the principle that allows objects of different classes to be treated as instances of a shared superclass or as conforming to a common protocol. It enables objects to exhibit different behaviors while responding to the same method call. Polymorphism enhances code flexibility and extensibility, allowing for interchangeable usage of objects based on their shared characteristics.

Abstraction is the principle of simplifying complex systems by representing essential features while hiding unnecessary details. It focuses on capturing the relevant attributes and behaviors of objects, allowing developers to create abstract representations that can be used as templates for concrete objects. Abstraction promotes code modularity, understandability, and scalability by providing a high-level view of the system's components.

Composition is the principle of building complex objects by combining simpler objects or components. It allows objects to be composed of other objects, forming a hierarchy of interconnected entities. Composition promotes code reuse and flexibility by creating relationships between objects through aggregation or containment. It enables the creation of larger and more specialized objects by combining smaller building blocks.

Association is the principle of establishing relationships between objects, representing how objects interact with each other. Associations can be one-to-one, one-to-many, or many-to-many, depending on the nature of the relationship. Associations facilitate communication and collaboration between objects, allowing them to exchange data and invoke each other's methods.

Classes, Objects, and Instances

Classes, objects, and instances are fundamental concepts in object-oriented programming that form the backbone of software development. They provide a powerful mechanism for creating reusable code, modeling real-world entities, and implementing complex systems. Most discussions of these begin with the concept of a class.

Classes

A class is a blueprint or a template that defines the properties and methods common to a particular type of object. It encapsulates data and behavior, serving as a foundation for creating instances. Classes support inheritance, allowing for the creation of hierarchical relationships and facilitating code reuse.

swift

```
class Person {
    var name: String
    var age: Int
    init(name: String, age: Int) {
        self.name = name
        self.age = age
    }
    func greet() {
        print("Hello, \(name) your password is \(age) days old.")
    }
}
```

This example defines a `Person` class with `name` and `age` properties and a `greet()` method. The `init` method initializes the properties when creating an instance of the class.

Objects and Instances

An object is an instance of a class. It represents a specific occurrence or realization of the class, possessing its own unique set of property values and state. Objects can be created by calling a class initializer.

swift

```
let john = Person(name: "John", age: 25)
john.greet() // Outputs: "Hello, John your password is 25 days old."
```

In this example, `john` is an object or instance of the `Person` class. We create an instance by calling the initializer of the class and pass in the desired property values.

Classes define the blueprint or structure of objects, specifying their properties and methods. When an instance of a class is created, it becomes an object, representing a specific occurrence or realization of that class. Multiple instances of the same class can exist, each with its own state and behavior.

Defining Structs and Classes

Structs and classes are two fundamental data types. They are used to create custom data types that can represent a variety of things, such as data models, UI elements, and game objects. For the most part, use structs by default. Structs are simpler and more efficient than classes. Structs are value types and classes are reference types.

There are some cases where a class is preferred. For example, use a class to

- Implement inheritance
- Control the identity of an object
- Implement a protocol that relies on reference semantics
- Use a mutable reference type

When unsure whether to use a struct or a class, it is best to err on the side of caution and use a struct.

Structs

Structs are value types, which means they are copied whenever they are assigned to a new variable or passed to a function. Structs are typically used to represent data models or lightweight objects that do not need to be modified frequently.

To define a struct, use the struct keyword followed by the name of the struct and a pair of curly braces. Inside the curly braces, define the properties of the struct. For example, the following code shows how to define a struct to represent a person, as used earlier:

swift

```
struct Person {
  var name: String
  var age: Int
}
```

This struct has two properties: name and age (or at least the age of their password). To create an instance of a struct, you use the initializer syntax. For example, the following code shows how to create an instance of the Person struct:

swift

```
let person = Person(name: "Charles", age: 59)
```

Once there's an instance of a struct, access the properties of the struct using the dot operator. The following shows how to access the name property of the person variable, using dot notation:

swift

```
let name = person.name
```

The next way many objects are defined is using a class.

Classes

Classes are reference types, which means that they are not copied when they are assigned to a new variable or passed to a function. Instead, a reference to the object is copied. Classes are typically used to represent complex objects that need to be modified frequently.

To define a class, use the class keyword followed by the name of the class and a pair of curly braces. Inside the curly braces, define the properties and methods of the class. The following shows how to define a class to represent a person:

swift

```
class Person {
  var name: String = ""
  var age: Int = 0
  func greet() {
    print("Hello, \(name) your password is \(age) days old.")
  }
}
```

This class has two properties: name and age. It also has a method called greet(), which prints a greeting to the console. To create an instance of a class, use the initializer syntax. For example, the following shows how to create an instance of the Person class:

swift

```
let person = Person()
```

Once an instance of a class is created, access the properties and methods of the class with the dot operator or using dot notation as was done in the section on structs. For example, the following code shows how to access the name property of the person variable:

swift

```
let name = person.name
```

You can also call the greet() method on the person variable:

swift

```
person.greet()
```

There are a number of different types of classes and structures. The first one covered is a memberwise struct.

Memberwise Structs

Memberwise structs are structs that have a memberwise initializer. A memberwise initializer is an initializer that initializes each property of the struct with the corresponding value from the initializer parameters. Memberwise structs are automatically generated by the Swift compiler for structs that do not have any custom initializers.

If you add your own custom initializer, Swift may stop generating the memberwise initializer automatically. Memberwise initializers can be useful in a variety of situations, for example, to create structs that represent data models or to create structs that represent the state of a UI element.

Properties and Methods

Properties and methods are fundamental components of object-oriented programming in any language. They encapsulate data and behavior within classes, structs, and enums.

Properties in Swift

Properties are variables or constants that associate values with a particular class, struct, or enum. They encapsulate data and state within an instance, enabling access, modification, and observation. Properties can be classified into two types: stored properties and computed properties.

Stored Properties

Stored properties are variables or constants that store a value directly as part of an instance. They can be defined within a class or struct and have their own memory allocation.

swift

```
struct Rectangle {
    var width: Double
    var height: Double
}
```

In this example, `width` and `height` are stored properties of the `Rectangle` struct.

Stored Properties of Constant Structures

Structures can have both stored and computed properties. Stored properties store a value for the instance of the structure, while computed properties calculate a value on the fly. When a structure instance is declared with `let`, its stored properties cannot be modified after initialization, even if those properties are declared with `var` in the type definition.

To declare immutable stored properties at the type level, use the `let` keyword instead of the `var` keyword. For example, the following code declares a `Point` structure with two immutable stored properties, `x` and `y`:

swift

```
struct Point {
  let x: Int
  let y: Int
}
```

Once a constant structure is declared, initialize an instance of the structure and assign values to its stored properties. For example, the following code initializes an instance of the Point structure:

swift

```
let point = Point(x: 10, y: 20)
```

Values of the stored properties of a constant structure cannot be modified once the instance has been initialized. For example, the following code will not compile:

swift

```
point.x = 30
```

If you need a value that is derived from other state and updates automatically, use a computed property.

Computed Properties

Computed properties do not store a value directly but provide a getter and an optional setter to calculate and return a value dynamically. Computed properties are defined using `get` and `set` blocks:

swift

```
struct Circle {
    var radius: Double
    var diameter: Double {
        get {
            return radius * 2
        }
        set {
            radius = newValue / 2
        }
    }
}
```

In this example, `diameter` is a computed property of the `Circle` struct. It calculates the diameter based on the radius and provides a setter to update the radius when the diameter is modified.

Read-Only Computed Properties

Read-only computed properties are properties that can be read but cannot be set. They are calculated based on the other properties of the class or struct. For example, the fullName property in the above example is a calculated value. Read-only computed properties can also be used to validate the values of other properties, for example, to create a read-only computed property that returns the error message for a property if the property is invalid.

Read-only computed properties can be used to create read-only views of other properties. For example, it's possible to create a read-only computed property that returns a formatted version of a string property. Keep in mind that the getter for a read-only computed property is executed every time the property is accessed and so can come with a performance impact and should be used sparingly. When accessing the value of a read-only computed property frequently, you should cache the value in a variable.

To declare a read-only computed property, use the var keyword followed by the name of the property and a colon. Then specify the getter for the property in curly braces. For example, the following code shows a read-only computed property for a class called Person:

swift

```
class Person {
  var name: String
  var age: Int
  init(name: String, age: Int) {
    self.name = name
    self.age = age
  }
  var fullName: String {
    return "\(name) has a password that is \(age) days old."
  }
}
```

The fullName property in the above example is a read-only computed property. It is calculated based on the name and age properties.

To access the value of a read-only computed property, you simply use the dot operator followed by the name of the property. For example, the following code shows how to access the value of the fullName property:

swift

```
let person = Person(name: "Alice", age: 25)
print(person.fullName) // Prints "Alice has a password that is 25
days old."
```

Another way to use a property is to summon a lazy stored property.

Lazy Stored Properties

Lazy stored properties have an initial value that is not calculated until the first time it is used. This can be useful for properties that are expensive to initialize or for properties that are not needed until a certain point in the program's execution. For example, use a lazy stored property to initialize a database connection or to load a large file into memory. Lazy stored properties can also be used to initialize properties that are not needed until a certain point in an app's execution. For example, use a lazy stored property to initialize a view that is only displayed when the user taps on a button. Lazy stored properties can also be used to provide default values for properties. For example, when using a lazy stored property to initialize a property with an empty value.

Deferring the initialization of expensive properties until they are needed can improve the startup performance of software and reduce the amount of memory used. However, lazy stored properties can make code more complex, especially if there are a lot of lazy stored properties in a single class or struct. Lazy stored properties are also not thread-safe. This means it is possible for the property to be initialized multiple times accidentally, which can actually slow software down and lead to unexpected behaviors.

Be a little careful with lazy stored properties as they do increase complexity in your code, plus there is a slight performance hit as the property has to be checked on each use to see if it has already been initialized.

To declare a lazy stored property, use the lazy keyword before the var keyword. For example, the following code shows a lazy stored property for a class called Person:

swift

```
class Person {
  let name: String
  let age: Int
  init(name: String, age: Int) {
    self.name = name
```

```
    self.age = age
  }
  lazy var fullName: String = "\(name) \(age)"
}
```

The fullName property in the above example is a lazy stored property. It is initialized the first time the fullName property is accessed.

To access the value of a lazy stored property, you simply use the dot operator followed by the name of the property. For example, the following code shows how to access the value of the fullName property:

swift

```
let person = Person(name: "Charles", age: 55)
print(person.fullName) // Prints "Charles 55"
```

The first time the `fullName` property is accessed, its initializer expression runs. The resulting string is then stored in `fullName` and returned to the caller.

Getter and Setter Syntax

Computed properties use `get` and `set` accessors. For read-only computed properties, Swift provides a concise form where you can omit `get` when there is only a single expression:

swift

```
struct Circle {
  var radius: Double
  var diameter: Double { radius * 2 }
}
```

For read-write computed properties, use both `get` and `set` (where `newValue` is provided automatically):

swift

```
struct Person {
  private var nameStorage = ""
  var name: String {
```

```
    get { nameStorage }
    set { nameStorage = newValue }
  }
}
```

These forms are commonly used for computed properties of many types, including Int, String, and Double.

Property Observers

Property observers are a way to monitor and respond to changes in the value of a property. They can be used to perform tasks such as updating the UI, saving data to disk, or logging changes to the console. This allows developers to use property observers to update a UI when the value of a property is changed, for example, to update the text label in a text field when the value of the text field's text property is changed. Property observers can also be used to save data to disk when the value of a property is changed, for example, to save the current state of a game to disk when the player saves the game. Property observers can also be used to log changes to the console when the value of a property is changed, like to log the current state of an app to the console when the player makes a move.

Property observers then help to decouple code by making it easier to separate the code that responds to property changes from the code that manages the property itself. Property observers can also make it clear how and when property changes are handled within code and surface property changes without the need to modify the code that manages a property.

There are two types of property observers in Swift. `willSet` observers are called just before the value of a property is changed. `didSet` observers are called just after the value of a property has been changed. To declare a property observer, attach `willSet` and/or `didSet` blocks directly to a stored property declaration.

For example, the following code shows a stored property with observers:

swift

```
struct Person {
  var name: String {
    willSet {
      print("The name is about to be changed from \(name) to \(newValue).")
    }
```

```
    didSet {
      print("The name was changed from \(oldValue) to \(name).")
    }
  }
}
```

The willSet observer in the above example is called just before the value of the name property is changed. The observer code prints a message to the console indicating that the name is about to be changed. To use a property observer, you simply declare the property observer and then access the property. The property observer will be called when the value of the property is changed. For example, the following code shows how to use the willSet observer from the above example:

swift

```
var person = Person(name: "Alice")
person.name = "Bob"
```

When the value of the name property is changed, the observers are called and messages are printed to the console.

The name is about to be changed from Alice to Bob.

The name was changed from Alice to Bob.

Property Wrappers

Property wrappers are a way to add extra functionality to properties. They can be used to constrain the values of properties, add validation, or provide other custom behavior. Property wrappers can encapsulate common functionality and so make code more easily reusable. For example, a property wrapper can be used to constrain the value of any property, regardless of its type. Property wrappers also make code more maintainable. For example, when adding a new property wrapper to validate a user's email address, simply create a new property wrapper and use it to wrap the email property.

There are a number of property wrappers, including `@NSCopying` (Foundation), wrappers commonly used in SwiftUI (such as `@State` and `@Binding`), and `@Published` from Combine.

To use a property wrapper, declare it using the `struct`, `enum`, or `class` keyword, followed by the `@propertyWrapper` attribute. Once a property wrapper is declared, use it to wrap a property by adding the @ symbol followed by the name of the property wrapper before the name of the property. For example, the following code shows how to declare and use a property wrapper to constrain the value of a property to a certain range:

swift

```
@propertyWrapper
struct Clamped<Value: Comparable> {
  private var range: ClosedRange<Value>
  private var value: Value
  init(wrappedValue: Value, range: ClosedRange<Value>) {
    self.value = wrappedValue
    self.range = range
  }
  var wrappedValue: Value {
    get { value }
    set { value = clamp(newValue, to: range) }
  }
  private func clamp(_ value: Value, to range: ClosedRange<Value>)
-> Value {
    if value < range.lowerBound {
      return range.lowerBound
    } else if value > range.upperBound {
      return range.upperBound
    } else {
      return value
    }
  }
}
class Person {
  @Clamped(range: 0...150) var age = 0
}
```

In the above example, the `Clamped` property wrapper is used to constrain the value of the age property to the range `0...150`. This means that the age property can never be less than `0` or greater than `150`. Property wrappers are a language feature used by many libraries and frameworks. For example, `@Published` (Combine) is often used with SwiftUI to publish model changes. Property wrappers can have unintended consequences as codebases grow, so sometimes it's good to protect values of other objects from them.

Private Property Wrappers

To restrict access when using property wrappers, apply access control to the wrapped property (and optionally the wrapper type). A wrapper's `wrappedValue` can define custom `get` and `set` behavior, which controls how the wrapped value is read and written.

For example, the following code shows how to protect the value of a property wrapper using a private property wrapper:

swift

```
@propertyWrapper
private struct Clamped<Value: Comparable> {
  private var range: ClosedRange<Value>
  private var value: Value
  init(wrappedValue: Value, range: ClosedRange<Value>) {
    self.value = wrappedValue
    self.range = range
  }
  var wrappedValue: Value {
    get { value }
    set { value = clamp(newValue, to: range) }
  }
  private func clamp(_ value: Value, to range: ClosedRange<Value>)
  -> Value {
    if value < range.lowerBound {
      return range.lowerBound
    } else if value > range.upperBound {
      return range.upperBound
    } else {
      return value
```

In this example, `square(_:)` is a type method of the `MathUtils` class. It calculates the square of a given number without requiring an instance of the class. Properties encapsulate data and state within instances, while methods provide functionality and behavior. Of the types of properties most developers need to interact with routinely, one of the most important to understand is the `self` property.

Self Property

The `self` keyword refers to the current instance of a type (class, struct, or enum). It can be used to access the properties and methods of the current instance and to disambiguate names. Using `self` can make code clearer in contexts where explicitness helps.

The `self` keyword is implicitly available in instance methods, initializers, and computed properties. It is not necessary to declare it explicitly. In the following example, we create a class called `User` and then call `self.name` rather than `name`:

swift

```
class User {
  var name: String
  init(name: String) {
    self.name = name
  }
  func login() {
    print("\(self.name) has logged in")
  }
}
let user = User(name: "Charles")
user.login() // Prints "Charles has logged in"
```

In the above example, the `login()` method uses `self` to access the `name` property of the current instance. To call a superclass initializer in a subclass initializer, use `super`, as shown in the following example:

swift

```
class Marketing: User {
  override init(name: String) {
    super.init(name: name)
  }
}
```

In the above example, the init() method for the Marketing class uses the super keyword to call the init() method of the User class. This ensures that the name property of the Marketing instance is initialized.

Mutating Methods

Mutating methods can change the value of the instance on which they are called. They are used with value types (structs and enums) when a method needs to modify `self` or one of its properties.

To declare a mutating method, use the mutating keyword before the func keyword. For example, the following code shows a mutating method:

swift

```
struct UserProfile {
  var name: String
  mutating func setName(to name: String) {
    self.name = name
  }
}
```

The `setName()` method in the above example is a mutating method because it can change the value of the `name` property of the `UserProfile` instance on which it is called. The `mutating` keyword is only used for value types such as structs and enums. Class instance methods can modify class properties without `mutating` because classes use reference semantics.

Here is an example of how to use a mutating method:

swift

```
var user = UserProfile(name: "Charles")
user.setName(to: "Elric")
print(user.name) // Prints "Elric"
```

In the above example, we call the setName() method to change the value of the name property of the user instance. After calling the setName() method, the name property of the user instance is equal to "Elric".

Class Inheritance and Subclasses

Inheritance is a key feature of object-oriented programming that allows a class to inherit properties, methods, and other characteristics from a superclass. The superclass serves as a base or template from which subclasses are derived. A class can inherit from only a single superclass, but it can be a superclass to multiple subclasses.

Class inheritance is used to create a new class based on an existing class. The new class is called the subclass, and the existing class is called the superclass. The subclass inherits all of the properties and methods of the superclass and can also add its own properties and methods, for example, to create a `Device` class that can then be used to create any type of device class, such as mobile, Mac, and Apple TV. This does cause classes to be tightly coupled and therefore can make changes more difficult without impacting other classes.

To create a subclass, you declare the subclass followed by a colon (`:`) and the superclass. For example, the following code shows an `iPhone` subclass of a `Device` class:

swift

```
class Device {
  func powerOn() {
    print("Powering on...")
  }
}

class iPhone: Device {
  // ...
}
```

The iPhone class inherits all of the properties and methods of the Device class. This means that iPhone objects can access and use all of the properties and methods that are defined in the Device class. For example, the following code shows how to create an iPhone object and call the powerOn() method:

swift

```
let iphone = iPhone()
iphone.powerOn()
```

The powerOn() method is defined in the Device class, but the iPhone object is able to call it because it is a subclass of the Device class.

Subclasses can also override the properties and methods of their superclasses. This allows you to customize the behavior of the subclass without having to modify the superclass itself. For example, the following code shows how to override the powerOn() method in the iPhone class:

swift

```
class iPhone: Device {
  override func powerOn() {
    print("Powering on iPhone...")
  }
}
```

Now, when calling the powerOn() method on an iPhone object, it will print "Powering on iPhone..." instead of using the superclass implementation.

Defining a Subclass

To create a subclass, use the colon (:) followed by the name of the superclass in the class declaration. The subclass inherits all the properties and methods defined in the superclass and can provide its own additional functionality or override inherited behavior.

swift

```
class Encryption {
    var speed: Double = 0.0
    func accelerate() {
        // Acceleration logic
    }
}
class FDE: Encryption {
    var brand: String = ""
    func escrow() {
        // Escrow logic
    }
}
```

In this example, the `Encryption` class is the superclass, and the `FDE` class is a subclass that inherits from `Encryption`. The `FDE` class adds a new property `brand` and a method `escrow()`.

Designated Initializers

Designated initializers are the primary initializers for a class. They are responsible for initializing all of the stored properties of a class and calling the appropriate superclass initializer to continue the initialization process up the superclass chain. Every class must have at least one designated initializer, but it can have multiple. It is common for a class to have a single designated initializer, but there are cases where it may be necessary to have multiple designated initializers.

Designated initializers can help ensure that all of the stored properties of a class are initialized before any other code is executed. This can help to prevent errors from occurring and make it easier to reason about the state of a class object. When all of the stored properties of a class are initialized, it is clear what state the object is in, especially when writing unit tests. This is especially important for classes that have complex initialization logic or that need to be in a known state before they can be used.

Designated initializers can be declared using the init() keyword. For example, the following code shows a class with a designated initializer:

swift

```
class Encrypt {
  var name: String
  init(name: String) {
    self.name = name
  }
}
```

This designated initializer initializes the name property of the Encrypt class. To call a designated initializer, you create an instance and pass the arguments required by the initializer. For example, the following code shows how to call the designated initializer for the Encrypt class:

swift

```
let encrypt = Encrypt(name: "Macintosh HD")
```

This will create a new Encrypt object with the name "Macintosh HD".

Designated initializers can also be inherited from superclasses. When a subclass inherits a designated initializer from its superclass, it can also override that initializer. However, when a subclass overrides a designated initializer, it must call the superclass's initializer before performing its own initialization.

Here is an example of a subclass that overrides a designated initializer:

swift

```
class Volume: Encrypt {
  var filesystem: String
  override init(name: String) {
    self.filesystem = "Apple_HFS"
    super.init(name: name)
  }
  init(name: String, filesystem: String) {
    self.filesystem = filesystem
    super.init(name: name)
  }
}
```

The Volume class overrides the designated initializer from the Encrypt class and also has a second designated initializer that initializes both the name and filesystem properties.

To call the overridden designated initializer for the Volume class, you simply create an instance of `Volume`:

swift

```
let volume = Volume(name: "Macintosh HD")
```

This will create a new Volume object with the name "Macintosh HD" and the filesystem "Apple_HFS".

To call the second designated initializer for the Volume class, you provide both arguments. For example:

swift

```
let volume = Volume(name: "iOS_21A5317a", filesystem: "GUID_partition_
scheme")
```

This will create a new Volume object with the name "iOS_21A5317a" and the filesystem as "GUID_partition_scheme". This could be used to surface simulator volumes attached to a Mac.

Convenience Initializers

Convenience initializers are secondary initializers that can call designated initializers to perform their initialization. They are used to provide additional ways to create instances of a class, often with simplified or more specific APIs. Convenience initializers can make it easier to create instances of a class by providing additional ways to do so.

Convenience initializers are declared using the convenience init() keyword. For example, the following code shows a class with a convenience initializer:

swift

```
import Foundation

class Volume {
  var name: String
  init(name: String) {
    self.name = name
  }
  convenience init() {
    self.init(name: NSUserName())
  }
}
```

The first initializer in this example is a designated initializer that initializes the name property of the Volume class. The second initializer is a convenience initializer that uses a global current-user value, which is useful in Mac sysadmin tooling where you may already have session context.

swift

```
let volume = Volume()
```

This creates a new `Volume` object with the name returned by `NSUserName()`, without having to pass `init(name:)` explicitly.

Convenience initializers can be inherited from superclasses under Swift's initializer inheritance rules. Subclasses can also define their own convenience initializers, which must delegate to another initializer in the same class.

Two-Phase Initializers

Two-phase initialization is a process that allows initializers to be performed in two phases. In phase 1, all of the stored properties of the class are initialized. In phase 2, any additional initialization that needs to be performed is done. This helps to ensure that all of the stored properties of the class are initialized before any other code is executed. This is especially important for classes that have complex initialization logic or that need to be in a known state before they can be used.

Ensuring that all of the stored properties of a class are initialized before any other code is executed helps prevent errors from occurring. When all of the stored properties of a class are initialized, it is clear what state the object is in. Two-phase initialization can help to make code more testable by making it easier to write unit tests for classes. When all of the stored properties of a class are initialized, there's certainty about the known state of a class before unit tests begin. Still, as with many of the Swift features covered in this book, two-phase initializers can make software more verbose and therefore more complex.

Two-phase initialization happens during class initialization. In phase 1, each class initializes its own stored properties before delegating to `super.init`. After the top of the inheritance chain has completed phase 1, phase 2 allows each class to further customize the instance.

In the second phase of initialization, the init() method can perform any additional initialization that needs to be done. This might include setting up dependencies, configuring the object, or validating the state of the object.

swift

```
class User {
  var name: String
  var devices: Int
  init(name: String, devices: Int) {
    self.name = name
    self.devices = devices
```

```
    // Perform additional initialization
    print("User created!")
  }
}
```

When an instance of the User class is created, the init() method is called. The initializer sets up stored properties and can then perform any additional initialization such as printing a message.

Initializer Inheritance

Initializers can be inherited from superclasses, but initializer inheritance follows specific rules. This can allow reuse of initialization logic from a superclass.

When a subclass inherits a designated initializer from its superclass, it can also override that initializer. However, when a subclass overrides a designated initializer, it must call the superclass's initializer before performing its own initialization.

Initializer inheritance and overriding follow specific rules. Here is an example:

swift

```
class Device {
  var name: String
  init(name: String) {
    self.name = name
  }
}
class iPhone: Device {
  var model: String
  init(name: String, model: String) {
    self.model = model
    super.init(name: name)
  }
}
```

In this example, the iPhone class calls the designated initializer from the Device class and adds its own stored property (`model`). Here is an example of how to use the iPhone class:

swift

```
let iphone = iPhone(name: "iPhone", model: "iPhone 16 Pro")
print(iphone.name) // Prints "iPhone"
print(iphone.model) // Prints "iPhone 16 Pro"
```

In this example, we create a new iPhone object by calling its initializer. The initializer initializes both the name and model properties.

Inheriting and Extending Functionality

Inheritance allows subclasses to inherit properties, methods, and initializers from the superclass, reducing code duplication. Subclasses can also add new properties and methods and override existing ones to provide specialized behavior.

swift

```
let myIPhone = iPhone(name: "iPhone", model: "iPhone 16 Pro")
print(myIPhone.name)  // Inherited from Device
print(myIPhone.model) // Specific to iPhone
```

In this example, we create an instance and call methods on it.

Access Control

Access control modifiers (`public`, `internal`, `private`, etc.) can be used to restrict or allow access to superclass members in subclasses. This provides control over which parts of the superclass are visible or modifiable in subclasses.

Inheritance and subclasses play a crucial role in object-oriented programming, enabling code reuse, extensibility, and hierarchical relationships between classes. Subclasses inherit properties, methods, and initializers from their superclasses, allowing for modular and reusable code design. By understanding and utilizing inheritance and subclasses effectively, developers can create well-organized, maintainable, and scalable code.

Failable Initializers, Propagation, and Overrides

A failable initializer is an initializer that can return `nil` instead of an instance. A call to a failable initializer therefore produces an optional result. Failable initializers are used when initialization can fail due to invalid or missing input.

To declare a failable initializer, use the init?() keyword. For example, the following code shows a failable initializer for a User class:

swift

```
class User {
  var name: String?
  var devices: Int?
  init?(name: String?, devices: Int?) {
    if let name = name, let devices = devices, devices >= 0 {
      self.name = name
      self.devices = devices
    } else {
      return nil
    }
  }
}
```

This initializer will fail if the given name is nil or the given devices value is less than 0. To call a failable initializer, call it like any other initializer and handle the optional result. For example, the following code shows how to call the init?() initializer for the User class:

swift

```
if let user = User(name: "Charles", devices: 5) {
  print(user.name ?? "Unknown") // Prints "Charles"
} else {
  print("Failed to create user.")
}
```

If the initializer fails, the result will be nil.

Propagation of initialization failure means that when a failable initializer fails, the initialization failure is propagated to the caller of the initializer. This means that the caller of the initializer must also be a failable initializer or handle the initialization failure. For example, the following code shows a failable initializer for a LoginManager class:

swift

```
class LoginManager {
```

```
  init?(user: User?) {
    if let user = user {
      // ...
    } else {
      return nil
    }
  }
}
```

This initializer will fail if the given user is nil. The following code shows how to call the init?() initializer for the LoginManager class:

swift

```
let user = User(name: "Charles", devices: 5)
if let loginManager = LoginManager(user: user) {
  // ...
} else {
  print("Failed to create login manager.")
}
```

If the init?() initializer for the LoginManager class fails, the result will be nil.

Failable initializers can be overridden in a subclass as well. When doing so, the superclass's initializer must be called. If the superclass's initializer fails, the initializer must also fail. For example, the following code shows how to override the init?() initializer for the LoginManager class in a subclass:

swift

```
class MyLoginManager: LoginManager {
  override init?(user: User?) {
    // Do some additional validation
    super.init(user: user)
  }
}
```

If the `init?()` initializer for the `MyLoginManager` class fails, the initializer will also fail. Keep in mind that a failable initializer cannot override a non-failable initializer, and if the superclass's initializer fails, the initializer must also fail.

Preventing Overrides

It is possible to prevent overriding for methods, properties, and subscripts. Preventing overrides can help to ensure that important methods and properties behave in a consistent way, even across different subclasses. Preventing overrides can help to protect code from being modified in unexpected ways and improve the performance of your code by allowing the compiler to optimize certain operations.

Preventing overrides can make code less flexible, as it prevents subclasses from customizing important methods and properties. Preventing overrides can make code more difficult to maintain, as it can be difficult to figure out why a particular method or property cannot be overridden. Don't prevent overrides when providing subclasses with the flexibility to customize important methods or properties.

To prevent a method, property, or subscript from being overridden, simply add the final keyword before the method, property, or subscript's introducer keyword. For example, the following code shows a class with a final method:

swift

```
class Device {
  final func powerOn() {
    print("Powering on...")
  }
}
```

This method cannot be overridden by any subclasses of the Device class.

You can also use the final keyword to prevent a property or subscript from being overridden. For example, the following code shows a class with a final property:

swift

```
class Device {
  final var name = "Device"
}
```

This property cannot then be overridden by any subclasses of the Device class.

Polymorphism and Overriding Methods

Polymorphism and method overriding allow for flexible and extensible code design. These mechanisms enable developers to write more modular and reusable code. Polymorphism is the ability of an object to take on multiple forms. Polymorphism is achieved through class inheritance and protocol conformance. It allows objects of different types to be treated as instances of a common superclass or conforming to a shared protocol. This enables greater flexibility in writing code that can work with different objects interchangeably.

Method Overriding

Method overriding is a key feature of polymorphism that allows a subclass to provide its own implementation of a method that is already defined in its superclass. The subclass can customize the behavior of the inherited method while preserving the same interface. Method overriding is achieved by using the `override` keyword when defining a method in a subclass. The overridden method must have the same name, parameters, and return type as the superclass method it is replacing.

swift

```
class Device {
    func wipe() {
        print("The device is getting wiped.")
    }
}
class iPhone: Device {
    override func wipe() {
        print("The iPhone is getting wiped.")
    }
}
```

In this example, the `Device` class has a method `wipe()`. The `iPhone` class inherits from `Device` and overrides the `wipe()` method with its own implementation.

Using Polymorphism and Method Overriding

Polymorphism and method overriding work together to allow objects of different classes to be treated as instances of a shared superclass. This enables code to be written in a generic way that operates on a superclass or protocol type, while different subclasses provide their specific behavior.

swift

```
func startWiping(device: Device) {
    device.wipe()
}
let myDevice: Device = iPhone()
startWiping(device: myDevice) // Outputs: "The iPhone is getting wiped."
```

In this example, the `startWiping` function accepts a `Device` parameter. It can receive any object that is a subclass of `Device`, such as an instance of the `iPhone` class. Despite being passed as a `Device`, the `wipe()` method of the `iPhone` class is invoked, demonstrating polymorphic behavior (and so allowing for different behaviors for different types of devices).

Subscripts

Subscripts offer a way to access and modify the elements of a collection. They are similar to methods, but more concise and easier to read and write. To declare a subscript, use the subscript keyword followed by the index type and the element type. For example, the following code shows a subscript that can be used to access the elements of an array of integers:

swift

```
struct IntArray {
  var array: [Int]
  subscript(index: Int) -> Int {
    get {
      return array[index]
    }
```

```
    set {
      array[index] = newValue
    }
  }
}
```

This subscript can be used to access and modify the elements of the array using square brackets. For example, the following code shows how to access and modify the first element of the array:

swift

```
var array = IntArray(array: [1, 2, 3, 4, 5])
// Access the first element of the array
let firstElement = array[0]
// Modify the first element of the array
array[0] = 10
```

Subscripts can also be used to access the elements of a dictionary. For example, the following code shows a subscript that can be used to access the value for a given key in a dictionary:

swift

```
struct StringDictionary {
  var dictionary: [String: String]
  subscript(key: String) -> String? {
    get {
      return dictionary[key]
    }
    set {
      dictionary[key] = newValue
    }
  }
}
```

This subscript can be used to access and modify the values in the dictionary using square brackets. For example, the following code shows how to access and modify the value for the key "name":

swift

```
var dictionary = StringDictionary(dictionary: ["name": "Default",
"devices": "5"])
// Access the value for the key "name"
let name = dictionary["name"]
// Modify the value for the key "name"
dictionary["name"] = "Charles"
```

Subscripts can be used to access and modify the elements of any type that conforms to the Collection protocol. This includes arrays, dictionaries, sets, and strings. Subscripts can make your code more concise and easier to read and write. For example, the following code is more concise and easier to read than the equivalent code that uses a property:

swift

```
let array = [1, 2, 3, 4, 5]
// Using a subscript
let firstElementBySubscript = array[0]
// Using a property
let firstElementByProperty = array.first
```

Subscripts can include index and bounds checks depending on the collection type and optimization level. In practice, choose subscript syntax when it improves clarity, and measure performance in context when performance is a concern.

Cyclomatic Complexity

Cyclomatic complexity measures the number of independent paths in a codebase, representing the level of decision-making and branching within the program. It provides insights into the number of test cases needed for thorough code coverage and serves as an indicator of code readability and maintainability. A higher cyclomatic complexity suggests increased complexity and the potential for more bugs or difficulties in understanding and modifying the code.

Cyclomatic complexity can be calculated using several methods, with one commonly used approach being the McCabe Cyclomatic Complexity formula. The formula defines cyclomatic complexity as the number of decision points plus one. Decision points typically include conditional statements (if, switch), loop statements (for, while), and logical operators (&&, ||). Each decision point increments the cyclomatic complexity by one, representing an additional possible execution path.

Tools and Frameworks

Several tools and frameworks in the Swift ecosystem provide automated cyclomatic complexity analysis. Reducing cyclomatic complexity will help manage a number of aspects of growing codebases, including

- **Readability and maintainability**: A lower cyclomatic complexity indicates code that is easier to read, understand, and maintain. Code with reduced complexity tends to have fewer nested branches and is less prone to errors, leading to better overall code quality.
- **Testability**: Cyclomatic complexity serves as a useful metric for determining the number of test cases required for comprehensive code coverage. By reducing complexity, developers can create test suites that efficiently validate all possible execution paths.
- **Refactoring and modifiability**: High cyclomatic complexity can make code refactoring and modifications challenging. By identifying areas with complex control flow, developers can prioritize refactoring efforts and improve the overall modifiability and scalability of the codebase.
- **Maintainability at scale**: Simpler control flow can reduce regression risk and make long-term changes safer.

There are a number of ways to attack cyclomatic complexity above and beyond just being a good team of developers. Consider the following:

- **Simplify conditional logic**: Break down complex conditional statements into smaller, more manageable parts. Consider extracting conditions into separate methods or leveraging Swift's guard statements to reduce nesting.
- **Extract reusable functions**: Identify recurring patterns of code and extract them into separate functions or methods. This promotes code reuse and readability and reduces overall complexity.

- **Modularization**: Divide complex functions or classes into smaller, focused units. Encapsulate related functionality into separate modules, promoting separation of concerns and reducing interdependencies.
- **Tools**: Use tools to surface areas for improvement.

Xcode offers built-in code coverage reporting. For cyclomatic complexity, teams typically rely on third-party tools such as OCLint and SwiftLint (`https://github.com/realm/SwiftLint`), which includes a `cyclomatic_complexity` rule.

Note For those who have Objective-C bits in their code, check out OCLint at *`https://oclint.org`*.

Cyclomatic complexity serves as a valuable metric for assessing code complexity and aiding in the creation of maintainable and high-quality codebases no matter the language (but also specifically given how much can change from version to version in Swift, it makes sense to monitor in Swift). Regularly monitoring complexity metrics and applying strategies to reduce complexity can lead to more robust, scalable, and easier-to-maintain applications.

Automatic Reference Counting

Automatic Reference Counting (ARC) is a memory management feature that automatically manages the memory used by objects. This means there's no need to worry about manually deallocating objects, as ARC handles deallocation automatically. ARC works by keeping track of the number of references to an object. When an object has no references, it is deallocated.

There are three common reference relationships in ARC: strong references, weak references, and unowned references. Strong references keep an object alive until all strong references to it are gone. Weak references do not keep an object alive and are automatically set to `nil` when the object is deallocated. Unowned references also do not keep an object alive, but they are non-optional and are used only when the referenced object is expected to outlive the reference. By default, references are strong unless marked otherwise.

Create a weak reference to an object by using the weak keyword. For example:

swift

```
class MyObject {}

class Holder {
  var object: MyObject? = MyObject()
  weak var weakObject: MyObject?

  init() {
    weakObject = object
  }
}
```

In this example, the `Holder` class keeps a strong reference to a `MyObject` in `object` and a weak reference in `weakObject`. The weak reference does not keep the object alive, so if `object` is set to nil (and there are no other strong references), the object can be deallocated and `weakObject` will become nil.

Conclusion

This chapter covered a lot of ground, because object-oriented programming is less a single feature than a way of organizing code: classes as blueprints, objects as instances of those blueprints, and principles like encapsulation, inheritance, polymorphism, and composition governing how they relate. In Swift, the most consequential decision is often the first one - struct or class. Structs are value types that get copied on assignment, classes are reference types that get shared, and the guidance from this chapter holds throughout the rest of the book. Use a struct by default, and reach for a class when inheritance, identity, or reference semantics are actually needed. The chapter also introduced the machinery that makes types useful day to day: stored, computed, and lazy properties; property observers and property wrappers; instance, type, and mutating methods; and subscripts for collection-like access. Initialization is where Swift is stricter than many languages - designated and convenience initializers, two-phase initialization, and failable initializers all exist to guarantee that an object is fully formed before it is used, and the compiler enforces those rules rather than leaving them as conventions. Inheritance and method overriding enable polymorphism, with `final` available when a class or member should not be extended further.

Finally, remember the two topics that live at the edges of OOP but matter to every project: cyclomatic complexity, as a reminder that deep class hierarchies and branching logic have a measurable maintenance cost, and Automatic Reference Counting, which manages memory for class instances through strong, weak, and unowned references. None of this needs to be mastered at once - as noted at the start of the chapter, most developers grow into OOP naturally as their projects get bigger and small scripts turn into real applications.

The next chapter covers optionals and error handling.

CHAPTER 8

Optionals and Error Handling

Optionals are a way to represent the absence of a value. They are used when a value may not always be available. For example, consider an optional to represent things like a user's current location, which may not be available if the user's location services are turned off, or the name of a device or model, frustratingly also not always available to an application.

Optionals can be one of the hardest elements in Swift to wrap your head around. Once you do understand them, however, you will probably find yourself using them all the time. While languages like Java, Rust, and others have the concept of optionals, Swift embraces optionals with a passion. Being comfortable with optionals will generally make your code safer, as many common attacks on software involve null pointer exceptions which optionals pretty much eliminate.

Error handling is a way to handle errors that occur during the execution of your program. Errors can occur for a variety of reasons, such as a network connection failure or a file not being found. Error handling allows you to gracefully handle these errors and prevent your program from crashing. Here are some examples of how optionals and error handling can be used in Swift:

Optionals:

- To represent the user's current location, which may not always be available
- To represent the result of a function that may not always return a value

C. Edge et al., *Mastering Swift*, https://doi.org/10.1007/979-8-8688-2770-9_8

Error handling:

- To handle a network connection failure
- To handle a file not being found
- To handle a user input error

One of the most useful aspects of Swift is the ability to throw errors easily.

Throwing Errors

Throwing errors is a way to signal that something went wrong during the execution of a function or method. This can be useful for handling errors in a centralized way and preventing unexpected behavior. It's useful to throw an error when something goes wrong during the execution of a function or method that cannot be easily recovered from. For example, if a file cannot be opened or if a network request fails.

Do not throw an error for minor problems, such as a missing field in a form or a typo in user input. Instead, handle these problems gracefully and display a helpful error message to the user. To throw an error, use the `throw` keyword. For example, the following code shows how to throw a simple error:

swift

```
enum ArithmeticError: Error {
  case divisionByZero
}

func divide(numerator: Int, denominator: Int) throws -> Int {
  if denominator == 0 {
    throw ArithmeticError.divisionByZero
  }
  return numerator / denominator
}
```

This function throws an ArithmeticError.divisionByZero error if the denominator is zero. To catch an error thrown by a function or method, use a do-catch statement. For example, the following code shows how to catch the error thrown by the divide() function:

swift

```
do {
  let result = try divide(numerator: 10, denominator: 5)
  print(result) // Prints 2
} catch ArithmeticError.divisionByZero {
  // Handle the division by zero error
  print("Division by zero")
}
```

If the divide() function throws an ArithmeticError.divisionByZero error, the catch block will be executed.

Throwing errors can make code more verbose, because it involves adding do-catch statements to all of the code that calls functions or methods that can throw errors. Throwing errors can also impact the performance of code, because the compiler needs to generate code to handle errors. However, they can be incredibly useful. In practice, errors are thrown from functions and methods marked with `throws`.

Throwing Functions

Throwing functions are functions that can throw errors and work similarly to non-throwing functions. This means they can signal to the caller that something went wrong during their execution. Throwing functions are useful for handling errors in a centralized way. To mark a function as throwing, use the `throws` keyword in the function declaration. For example, the following code shows a throwing function that throws a FileNotFoundError error if the file at the specified path does not exist:

swift

```
func readFile(at path: String) throws -> String {
  // ...
}
```

To call a throwing function, use the `try` keyword. For example, the following code shows how to call the readFile() function:

swift

```
do {
  let fileContents = try readFile(at: "/path/to/devicedetails.plist")
```

```
  // ...
} catch FileNotFoundError.fileNotFound {
  // Handle the file not found error
}
```

If the readFile() function throws a FileNotFoundError error, the catch block will be executed. As with throwing errors, do not use throwing functions for minor problems, such as a missing field in a form or a typo in user input. Instead, handle these problems gracefully and display a helpful error message to the user.

Error Propagation

Error propagation allows errors to be thrown from one function to another. This can be useful for handling errors in a centralized way. When a function or method throws an error, the error is propagated to the calling function or method. This continues until the error is caught or it reaches the top of the call stack. If an error is never handled, the program terminates at runtime.

To use error propagation, mark the functions and methods that can throw errors with the throws keyword. For example, the following code shows how to mark a function that can throw a FileNotFoundError error:

swift

```
func readFile(at path: String) throws -> String {
  // ...
}
```

This function can throw an error if the file at the specified path does not exist. To call a function or method that can throw an error, you need to use the try keyword. For example, the following code shows how to call the readFile() function:

swift

```
do {
  let fileContents = try readFile(at: "/path/to/devicedetails.plist")
  // ...
} catch FileNotFoundError.fileNotFound {
  // Handle the file not found error
}
```

If the readFile() function throws a FileNotFoundError error, the catch block will be executed.

Converting Errors to Optionals with try?

The `try?` operator converts a throwing expression into an optional result. If the expression succeeds, you get a value. If it throws, you get `nil`, and the original error is discarded.

Use `try?` when treating failure as the absence of a value is appropriate. For example:

swift

```
func loadFile(at path: String) throws -> String {
  // ...
}
let fileContents = try? loadFile(at: "/path/to/devicedetails.plist")
if let fileContents {
  print(fileContents)
}
```

If `loadFile()` throws an error, `fileContents` is set to `nil`.

Do-Catch

The do-catch statement is used to handle errors that can be thrown by a function or method. It provides a structured way to catch and handle errors in your code. To use the do-catch statement, wrap the code that may throw an error in a do block. Then add one or more catch clauses to handle the different types of errors that can be thrown.

For example, the following code uses a do-catch statement to handle an error that can be thrown by the readFile() function:

swift

```
do {
  let contents = try readFile(at: "/path/to/devicedetails.plist")
  // Do something with the contents of the file.
} catch let error {
  // Handle the error.
}
```

The try keyword is used to indicate that the code in the do block may throw an error. If an error is thrown, the execution of the do block will stop, and the code in the catch clause will be executed. Use multiple catch clauses to handle different types of errors. For example, the following code uses two catch clauses to handle the two different types of errors that can be thrown by the readFile() function:

swift

```
do {
  let contents = try readFile(at: "/path/to/devicedetails.plist")
  // Do something with the contents of the file.
} catch let error as NSError where error.code == NSFileNoSuchFileError {
  // Handle the error that is thrown if the file does not exist.
} catch let error {
  // Handle any other error that is thrown.
}
```

It's also possible to use a catch clause to catch all types of errors. For example, the following code uses a single catch clause to catch all types of errors that can be thrown by the readFile() function:

swift

```
do {
  let contents = try readFile(at: "/path/to/devicedetails.plist")
  // Do something with the contents of the file.
} catch {
  // Handle any error that is thrown.
}
```

It is important to only use a catch clause to catch errors that you can handle gracefully. If an error cannot be handled gracefully, allow the error to propagate up the call stack.

Converting Throwing Calls to Optionals

Throwing functions do not represent failures as `Error?` by default. A throwing function returns its normal value type on success and throws on failure. If you want an optional result instead, you can use `try?` to convert T into T?. For example, the following code declares a function that can throw an error:

swift

```
func readFile(at path: String) throws -> String {
  // ...
}
```

The `throws` keyword indicates that the function can throw an error. If the function throws an error, the execution of the function will stop, and the error will be propagated up the call stack. To call `readFile()`, you can use either `do-catch` or `try?`, depending on whether you need detailed error information.

For example, the following code converts the throwing call into an optional:

swift

```
let contents = try? readFile(at: "/path/to/devicedetails.plist")
if let contents {
  // Do something with the contents of the file.
}
```

With `try?`, a thrown error becomes `nil`, and error details are not preserved.

Cleanup Actions

Error cleanup actions are actions that are performed when an error occurs. This can be useful for freeing up resources, closing files, or performing other cleanup tasks. Error cleanup actions can be performed using the defer statement or a custom error handler. The defer statement can be used to perform cleanup actions, regardless of how the code block exits. This means that the cleanup actions will be performed even if an error occurs.

To use the defer statement, wrap the code that needs to be cleaned up in a defer block. For example, the following code uses a defer statement to close a file:

swift

```
func readFile(at path: String) throws -> String {
  defer {
    // Close the file.
  }
```

```
  // ...
}
```

If an error occurs in the readFile() function, the defer block will still be executed, and the file will be closed. Also consider a custom error handler to perform error cleanup actions. To do so, implement a function that takes an error as a parameter and performs the necessary cleanup actions.

For example, the following code defines a custom error handler that closes a file:

swift

```
func closeFileHandler(error: Error) {
  // Close the file.
}
```

It's then possible to use the closeFileHandler() function to handle errors in code. For example, the following code calls the readFile() function and uses the closeFileHandler() function to handle the error that it can throw:

swift

```
func readFile(at path: String) throws -> String {
  // ...
}
do {
  let contents = try readFile(at: "/path/to/devicedetails.plist")
  // Do something with the contents of the file.
} catch let error {
  closeFileHandler(error: error)
}
```

If an error occurs in the readFile() function, the closeFileHandler() function will be called to close the file.

The best way to perform error cleanup actions depends on your specific needs. When performing cleanup actions, regardless of how the code block exits, it's usually best to use the `defer` statement. For more complex cleanup actions, or when performing different cleanup actions depending on the type of error that occurs, consider a custom error handler.

Dealing with Optional Values

Optional values represent the presence or absence of a value. They allow variables and constants to be explicitly marked as potentially containing nil. Optional values are denoted by appending a question mark (`?`) after the type declaration.

Optional unwrapping is the process of extracting the underlying value from an optional. There are multiple techniques for unwrapping optionals, including optional binding, forced unwrapping, and the nil coalescing operator. Optional binding is a safe way to unwrap an optional value and assign it to a new non-optional variable or constant within a specific scope. It involves using the `if let` or `guard let` construct to conditionally check for nil and perform further operations when the optional contains a value.

Forced unwrapping is a technique used when we are certain that an optional contains a value and want to access it directly. It involves using the exclamation mark (`!`) to forcefully unwrap the optional. However, caution should be exercised because forcing the unwrapping of a nil optional results in a runtime error.

Optional chaining provides an elegant way to access properties, methods, and subscripts of an optional value without explicitly unwrapping it. It allows developers to chain multiple optional operations together and gracefully handle situations where any link in the chain is nil.

The nil coalescing operator (`??`) provides a concise way to provide a default value for an optional when it evaluates to nil. It allows developers to specify a fallback value to use in case the optional is nil.

There are a few things to consider when dealing with optional values. Use optional binding (`if let` or `guard let`) to safely unwrap optionals and avoid runtime errors caused by accessing nil values. Also keep in mind that it's important to minimize forced unwrapping (`!`) and only use it when you are absolutely certain that the optional contains a value. Optional chaining allows safe access to properties and methods of nested optionals without explicitly unwrapping each level.

There's a lot that optional values provide, including bindings.

Optional Binding and Forced Unwrapping

Optionals represent values that may be absent or nil. They provide a type-safe way to handle situations where a value might be missing. An optional variable or constant is denoted by appending a question mark (?) after the type declaration.

Optional Binding

Optional binding is a technique used to safely unwrap an optional value and assign it to a new non-optional variable or constant within a specific scope. It allows us to check if an optional has a value and conditionally execute code based on its presence. The syntax of optional binding is as follows:

swift

```
if let unwrappedValue = optionalValue {
    // Code to execute when optionalValue is not nil
    // The unwrapped value is available as unwrappedValue
} else {
    // Code to execute when optionalValue is nil
}
```

Let's consider an example where we want to safely handle an optional username:

swift

```
let optionalUsername: String? = getUsername() // A function that returns an
optional username
if let username = optionalUsername {
    print("Welcome, \(username)!")
} else {
    print("Welcome, Guest!")
}
```

In this example, if `optionalUsername` is not nil, the value will be unwrapped and assigned to the non-optional constant `username`, allowing us to use it safely within the scope of the `if` statement. If `optionalUsername` is nil, the code within the `else` block will execute.

Forced Unwrapping

Forced unwrapping is a technique used when it's certain that an optional contains a value, and there's a need to access that value directly. It involves using the exclamation mark (`!`) to forcefully unwrap the optional.

The syntax of forced unwrapping is as follows:

swift

```
let unwrappedValue = optionalValue!
```

Consider an example where we have an optional number and we want to forcefully unwrap it:

swift

```
let optionalNumber: Int? = getNumber() // A function that returns an
optional number
let unwrappedNumber = optionalNumber!
print("The number is \(unwrappedNumber).")
```

In this example, we assume that `optionalNumber` contains a value. To use forced unwrapping, directly access the value of `optionalNumber` and assign it to `unwrappedNumber`. However, if `optionalNumber` is nil, a runtime error will occur.

Caution with forced unwrapping: It's important to exercise caution when using forced unwrapping because if the optional is nil, it will result in a runtime error. It is generally recommended to use optional binding to safely handle optionals and avoid forced unwrapping whenever possible. Force unwrapping eliminates all of the code safety that using optionals provides in the first place.

Optional binding allows us to conditionally unwrap an optional and use the value within a specific scope, while forced unwrapping provides a way to directly access the value when we are certain it exists. By understanding and utilizing these techniques, Swift developers can handle optionals effectively and write safer, more reliable code.

Forced Unwrapping vs. Optional Chaining

Sometimes developers use multiple ! operators in one expression to unwrap several optionals inline. It can make code concise, but it will crash at runtime if any unwrapped value is `nil`. For example:

swift

```
struct User {
  var profile: Profile?
}
struct Profile {
  var address: Address?
}
struct Address {
  var zipCode: String
}

let user: User? = User(profile: Profile(address: Address(zipCode:
"02139")))
// Force-unwrap a chain of optionals
let zipCode = user!.profile!.address!.zipCode
print(zipCode) // Prints "02139"
```

If any link in this chain is `nil` (`user`, `profile`, or `address`), the code crashes at the line where `zipCode` is read.

The same idea applies when calling a method on an optional object. This example uses forced unwrapping:

swift

```
struct Person {
  var name: String
  func greet() {
    print("Hello, my name is \(name).")
  }
}
var person: Person? = Person(name: "Charles")
// Forced unwrapping
person!.greet() // Prints "Hello, my name is Charles."
```

If `person` is `nil`, `person!.greet()` crashes. The safer alternative is optional chaining:

swift

```
person?.greet() // Calls greet() only when person is non-nil
```

Forced unwrapping can look concise, but optional binding is often safer when you need a value:

swift

```
// Forced unwrapping
let forcedZipCode = user!.profile!.address!.zipCode
// Optional binding
let safeZipCode: String
if let user, let profile = user.profile, let address = profile.address {
  safeZipCode = address.zipCode
} else {
  safeZipCode = "Unknown ZIP code"
}
```

Forced unwrapping can make code harder to reason about when many optionals are involved. Use forced unwrapping only when you are certain the value is non-nil.

Use regular optional unwrapping instead if you are unsure whether the optional values will always be present to help make code safer and more readable.

Nil Coalescing Operator

The nil coalescing operator (`??`) provides a concise and powerful way to handle optional values. It offers an elegant solution for dealing with cases where a value may be optional and provides a default value to use when the optional value is nil. In this article, we will explore the nil coalescing operator and learn how to leverage its functionality. Optionals allow variables and constants to represent the absence of a value. They provide a safer alternative to handling nil values and help prevent runtime crashes due to accessing nil objects. Optionals are denoted by appending a question mark (`?`) after the type declaration.

Syntax of the Nil Coalescing Operator

The nil coalescing operator (`??`) is a binary operator that allows us to provide a default value for an optional when it evaluates to nil. The syntax is as follows:

swift

```
optionalValue ?? defaultValue
```

If `optionalValue` is not nil, the expression evaluates to `optionalValue`. However, if `optionalValue` is nil, the expression evaluates to `defaultValue`. Let's consider an example where we want to assign a default name when a user's name is optional:

swift

```
let userName: String? = getUserInput() // A function that returns an
optional name
let displayName = userName ?? "Guest"
print("Welcome, \(displayName)!")
```

In this example, if `userName` contains a non-nil value, it will be assigned to `displayName`. Otherwise, if `userName` is nil, `displayName` will be set to "Guest".

Coalescing with Complex Types

The nil coalescing operator is not limited to simple types like strings. It can be used with any optional type, including complex types such as arrays, dictionaries, or custom objects:

swift

```
let optionalArray: [Int]? = getOptionalArray() // A function that returns
an optional array
let array = optionalArray ?? [1, 2, 3]
```

In this case, if `optionalArray` is not nil, it will be assigned to `array`. Otherwise, if `optionalArray` is nil, `array` will be assigned the default array `[1, 2, 3]`.

Chaining Nil Coalescing Operators

Multiple nil coalescing operators can be chained together to provide fallback values in a hierarchical manner. This allows for more complex default value handling.

swift

```
let optionalValue: Int? = getOptionalValue() // A function that returns an
optional value
let fallbackValue: Int? = getFallbackValue() // A function that returns an
optional fallback value
let defaultValue: Int = 0
let value = optionalValue ?? fallbackValue ?? defaultValue
```

In this example, if `optionalValue` is not nil, it will be assigned to `value`. If `optionalValue` is nil, the expression will evaluate `fallbackValue`. If `fallbackValue` is also nil, the expression will finally evaluate to `defaultValue`.

The nil coalescing operator (`??`) provides an elegant and concise way to handle optional values and assign default values when an optional evaluates to nil. By using the nil coalescing operator, developers can streamline their code and handle optional scenarios with ease. Whether dealing with simple types or complex objects, understanding and utilizing the nil coalescing operator empowers developers to write more robust and readable code.

Implicitly Unwrapped Optionals

An optional is a value that can be either present or absent. Optionals are used to represent values that may or may not be available, such as the result of a function that may fail or the value of a property that may not have been initialized yet.

An implicitly unwrapped optional is an optional that can be implicitly unwrapped when used in a context that expects a non-optional value. It is still an optional and can still be `nil`. To declare an implicitly unwrapped optional, use `!` after the type name. For example, the following code declares an implicitly unwrapped optional variable of type `String`:

swift

```
var name: String!
```

You can then assign a value to an implicitly unwrapped optional variable, just as you would assign a value to a regular variable. For example, the following code assigns the string "Charles" to the `name` variable:

swift

```
name = "Charles"
```

Once a value is assigned to an implicitly unwrapped optional variable, Swift can use it in places that expect a non-optional value. For example:

swift

```
func greet(name: String) {
  print("Hello, \(name)")
}

greet(name: name) // `name` is implicitly unwrapped here
```

Implicitly unwrapped optionals can be more convenient to use than regular optionals in specific cases, but they should be used carefully because accessing a nil value still causes a runtime crash. For example, you might use an implicitly unwrapped optional to represent a property value that is set up shortly after initialization. If you are unsure whether the value will always be present, use a regular optional instead. This will help make your code safer and more readable.

Throwing Functions and Handling Errors

Throwing functions allow developers to indicate that a function can potentially encounter an error during execution. By marking a function with the `throws` keyword in its declaration, it can throw an error. Throwing functions play a vital role in propagating errors and enabling proper error handling. Let's consider a simple example of a throwing function that performs a division operation:

swift

```
enum DivisionError: Error {
    case divisionByZero
}
func divide(_ dividend: Int, by divisor: Int) throws -> Int {
    guard divisor != 0 else {
        throw DivisionError.divisionByZero
    }
    return dividend / divisor
}
```

In this example, the `divide(_:by:)` function can throw a `DivisionError` if the divisor is zero. By throwing the error, it indicates that the division operation encountered an exceptional scenario.

Handling Errors with Do-Catch Blocks

To handle errors thrown by throwing functions, we use do-catch blocks. The do block contains the code that might throw an error, while the `catch` block allows us to handle specific types of errors. The syntax for a do-catch block in Swift is as follows:

swift

```
do {
    // Code that can potentially throw an error
    let result = try divide(10, by: 0)
    print("Result: \(result)")
} catch DivisionError.divisionByZero {
    // Handle the specific error case
    print("Cannot divide by zero.")
} catch {
    // Handle any other errors
    print("An error occurred: \(error)")
}
```

In this example, the do block attempts to divide 10 by 0 using the `divide(_:by:)` function. If a `DivisionError.divisionByZero` error is thrown, the first `catch` block handles that specific error case. The final `catch` block serves as a catch-all for any other errors.

Propagating Errors

Errors can be propagated from one function to another using the `throws` keyword. When calling a throwing function, the caller must handle the error by using the `try` keyword. If the error is not handled locally, it will be propagated up the call stack until it reaches an appropriate catch block.

swift

```
func performComplexCalculation() throws {
```

```
    let result = try divide(10, by: 0)
    // Perform other calculations
}
do {
    try performComplexCalculation()
} catch {
    print("An error occurred: \(error)")
}
```

In this example, the `performComplexCalculation()` function calls the `divide(_:by:)` function, which can throw a `DivisionError`. If the error is not handled within `performComplexCalculation()`, it will propagate up to the calling scope.

Sometimes, we may want to rethrow an error from within a catch block. This is useful to catch an error, perform some additional processing, and then propagate the error further. This is achieved when the `try` and `throw` keywords are used together.

Do-Catch Blocks and Error Propagation

Error handling is an essential mechanism that allows developers to gracefully handle exceptional situations and recover from errors during program execution. Do-catch blocks provide a structured approach to handle errors, while error propagation allows errors to be propagated up the call stack for centralized handling. In this article, we will delve into the concepts of do-catch blocks and error propagation in Swift.

Do-catch blocks provide a structured way to handle errors in Swift. They allow us to encapsulate code that may potentially throw an error and provide specific error handling logic. By utilizing do-catch blocks, we can catch and respond to errors, ensuring our code handles exceptional scenarios gracefully.

The basic syntax of a do-catch block in Swift is as follows:

swift

```
do {
    // Code that can potentially throw an error
    try someThrowingFunction()
} catch {
```

```
    // Error handling code
    print("An error occurred: \(error)")
}
```

Inside the do block, we place the code that might throw an error. If an error is thrown, it is caught by the `catch` block, where we can handle the error appropriately. The caught error is accessible using the implicit `error` constant, which provides information about the error. Error propagation allows errors to be passed from the point of occurrence to higher-level scopes for centralized error handling. By propagating errors up the call stack, we can handle them at a more suitable location in our codebase.

Throwing Functions and Methods

Functions and methods that can potentially throw an error are marked with the `throws` keyword in their declaration. This indicates that the function or method may produce an error that needs to be handled by the caller or propagated further up the call stack.

Here's an example of a function that throws an error:

swift

```
enum CustomError: Error {
    case somethingWentWrong
}
func performTask(shouldFail: Bool) throws {
    // Perform task that might throw an error
    if shouldFail {
        throw CustomError.somethingWentWrong
    }
}
```

The errors can then be propagated as well.

Error Propagation with Throwing Functions

When calling a throwing function, propagate the error by using the `try` keyword. If the function throws an error, it will be passed up the call stack until it is caught or handled by a do-catch block.

swift

```
do {
    try performTask(shouldFail: true)
} catch {
    // Handle the error here
    print("An error occurred: \(error)")
}
```

Error propagation can have multiple levels as well.

Conclusion

Error propagation can occur through multiple levels of function calls, with or without optionals. Each level can choose to handle the error locally or continue propagating it up the call stack until it reaches an appropriate catch block. It is not necessary to catch errors at every level; catch them where you can handle them meaningfully, and otherwise, let them propagate. Errors can then be logged, surfaced in debug consoles, or reported through crash reporting systems. This is part of writing quality code that is resilient and easier to maintain.

The next chapter covers structs, enums, and protocols.

CHAPTER 9

Structs, Enums, and Protocols

Structs, enums, and protocols are all fundamental types. They have different strengths and weaknesses, and the best choice for a particular task depends on its specific requirements and how the type will be used.

Structs are value types, which means that they are copied when they are passed around or assigned to a new variable. This makes them a good choice for data that does not need to be shared between different parts of your program. For example, consider a struct to represent a user's profile information.

Enums are a way to represent a set of possible values. They are a good choice for data that can have one of a limited number of possible values. For example, an enum might be useful to represent the different possible states of a user account.

Protocols are a way to define a blueprint for other types to follow. They can be used to enforce certain behavior or to allow different types to work together. For example, a protocol is useful for defining the behavior of a button.

In general, use each in the following manner:

- **Structs**: To represent data that does not need to be shared between different parts of a program
- **Enums**: To represent a set of possible values
- **Protocols**: To define a blueprint for other types to follow

These can overlap, and so only experience teaches good programmers when to use each. However, those are some good guidelines to get started. Now, let's investigate how each is used.

C. Edge et al., *Mastering Swift*, https://doi.org/10.1007/979-8-8688-2770-9_9

Using Structs to Define Value Types

A struct is a user-defined composite type that encapsulates data and behavior. It serves as a blueprint for creating instances that hold a collection of properties and methods. Unlike classes, which are reference types, structs are value types, meaning they are copied when assigned or passed around.

To define a struct in Swift, use the `struct` keyword followed by the name of the struct type. Within the struct's body, define its properties and methods. Here's an example of a simple struct representing a point in a 2D coordinate system:

swift

```
struct Point {
    var x: Int
    var y: Int
}
```

One of the key benefits of using structs is that they are value types. When a struct instance is assigned to a new variable or passed as a function parameter, a copy of the value is made. This behavior ensures that each instance has its own independent data, preventing unintended side effects. In practice, many structs are designed to be immutable where possible by using `let` properties. Immutability can improve thread safety and is often helpful in concurrent code.

Some standard-library value types that are structs, such as `Array`, `Dictionary`, and `String`, use copy-on-write optimizations behind the scenes to keep copying efficient. With copy-on-write, storage is shared until one copy is mutated, at which point a separate copy of the underlying storage is created. This means that with copy-on-write structs, if you make many copies but they are all only used for reading from the structure rather than mutating it, then the expensive work of physically making all of those copies can be avoided.

Structs exhibit value semantics, meaning they are copied by value rather than referenced by identity. Equality, however, is available only when the type conforms to `Equatable`.

Structs are often lightweight and efficient due to value semantics. They are a suitable choice for storing small to medium-sized data structures, such as coordinates, sizes, colors, and other value-based entities. Structs can be composed together to create more complex value types. By nesting structs or using them as properties, we can build hierarchies of value types that model various aspects of our domain.

Enumerations and Their Associated Values

Enumerations are typically used to define a finite set of related values under a single type. They provide a convenient way to represent a group of related options, states, or choices. Enums are particularly useful for ensuring type safety and improving code clarity by explicitly defining the available options.

To define an enumeration, use the enum keyword followed by the name of the enum type and a list of cases, each representing a distinct value within the enum. Here's an example:

swift

```
enum WiFiNetwork {
    case northCampus
    case southCampus
    case eastCampus
    case westCampus
}
```

Once defined, use enums to create instances of the defined type and work with their values. For example:

swift

```
let network: WiFiNetwork = .northCampus
```

Dot syntax can then be used in other parts of the code. Building on this concept, enums can also declare associated values and expose their data through pattern matching.

Associated Values

Associated values are a powerful feature of Swift enums that allow us to attach additional data to each enum case. This capability makes enums more flexible and enables them to represent a wide range of scenarios. To define associated values, we specify the data type(s) inside parentheses after each enum case. Here's an example of an enum representing different types of geometric shapes with associated values:

swift

```
enum Shape {
    case circle(radius: Double)
    case square(sideLength: Double)
    case rectangle(width: Double, height: Double)
}
```

When using enums with associated values, we can provide the necessary data when creating an instance of the enum. For example:

swift

```
let shape1 = Shape.circle(radius: 5.0)
let shape2 = Shape.square(sideLength: 10.0)
let shape3 = Shape.rectangle(width: 8.0, height: 6.0)
```

The associated values can then be passed into other code, such as using a switch statement to determine what an app should draw on the screen.

Accessing Associated Values

To access the associated values of an enum instance, use a `switch` statement or pattern matching. This allows us to extract and work with the associated data based on the enum case. Here's an example:

swift

```
switch shape1 {
case .circle(let radius):
    print("Circle with radius: \(radius)")
case .square(let sideLength):
    print("Square with side length: \(sideLength)")
case .rectangle(let width, let height):
    print("Rectangle with width: \(width) and height: \(height)")
}
```

Enumerations with associated values provide a powerful tool for modeling various scenarios and representing a range of values in a type-safe manner. By defining enums and attaching associated values, Swift developers can create expressive and flexible code that accurately represents the problem domain.

Enumeration Values with a Switch Statement

Enumerations are a way to define a named set of related values. They can be used to represent a variety of things, such as the different states of a machine, the different days of the week, or the different types of errors that an operation can return.

Switch statements in Swift can execute different code depending on the value of an expression. This can be useful for handling different enumeration values. For example, the following code shows a switch statement that handles the different days of the week:

swift

```
enum DayOfWeek {
  case monday
  case tuesday
  case wednesday
  case thursday
  case friday
  case saturday
  case sunday
}
let dayOfWeek = DayOfWeek.monday
switch dayOfWeek {
case .monday:
  print("It's Monday!")
case .tuesday:
  print("It's Tuesday!")
case .wednesday:
  print("It's Wednesday!")
case .thursday:
  print("It's Thursday!")
case .friday:
  print("It's Friday!")
case .saturday:
  print("It's Saturday!")
case .sunday:
  print("It's Sunday!")
}
```

This code prints the message "It's Monday!" because the value of the `dayOfWeek` variable is `DayOfWeek.monday`. You can also use switch statements to handle multiple enumeration values at once. For example, the following code shows a switch statement that handles the weekend days:

swift

```
enum DayOfWeek {
  case monday
  case tuesday
  case wednesday
  case thursday
  case friday
  case saturday
  case sunday
}
let dayOfWeek = DayOfWeek.saturday
switch dayOfWeek {
case .saturday, .sunday:
  print("It's the weekend!")
default:
  print("It's not the weekend.")
}
```

This code will print the message "It's the weekend!" because the value of the dayOfWeek variable is DayOfWeek.saturday.

When using switch statements with enumeration values, it is important to handle all possible cases. For your own enums, Swift usually requires exhaustive handling without a `default` case. For enums that may gain future cases (e.g., in external libraries), `@unknown default` can be used. You can also use the `where` keyword to filter the enumeration values handled by a switch statement.

Iterating over Enumerations

Enumerations are a way to define a named set of related values. They can be used to represent a variety of things, such as the different states of a machine, the different days of the week, or the different types of errors that an operation can return. A common way to iterate over all cases is to conform the enum to `CaseIterable` and loop over `allCases`. For example, the following code shows how to iterate over the `DayOfWeek` enum:

swift

```
enum DayOfWeek: CaseIterable {
  case monday
  case tuesday
  case wednesday
  case thursday
  case friday
  case saturday
  case sunday
}
for dayOfWeek in DayOfWeek.allCases {
  print(dayOfWeek)
}
```

This code prints the following output to the console:

swift

```
monday
tuesday
wednesday
thursday
friday
saturday
sunday
```

The `enumerated()` method returns a sequence of pairs, where each pair consists of an index and an element from a collection. For example, the following code shows how to use `enumerated()` with all `DayOfWeek` cases:

swift

```
enum DayOfWeek: CaseIterable {
  case monday
  case tuesday
  case wednesday
  case thursday
```

```
  case friday
  case saturday
  case sunday
}
for (index, dayOfWeek) in DayOfWeek.allCases.enumerated() {
  print("\(index): \(dayOfWeek)")
}
```

This code will print the following output to the console:

swift

```
0: monday
1: tuesday
2: wednesday
3: thursday
4: friday
5: saturday
6: sunday
```

The `map()` method applies a function to each element of an array (or other sequence) and returns an array containing the results. For example, the following code shows how to use `map()` to convert the `DayOfWeek` enum to a string array:

swift

```
enum DayOfWeek: CaseIterable {
  case monday
  case tuesday
  case wednesday
  case thursday
  case friday
  case saturday
  case sunday
}
let dayOfWeekStrings = DayOfWeek.allCases.map { (dayOfWeek: DayOfWeek) ->
String in
  switch dayOfWeek {
  case .monday:
```

```
    return "Monday"
  case .tuesday:
    return "Tuesday"
  case .wednesday:
    return "Wednesday"
  case .thursday:
    return "Thursday"
  case .friday:
    return "Friday"
  case .saturday:
    return "Saturday"
  case .sunday:
    return "Sunday"
  }
}
print(dayOfWeekStrings)
```

This code will print the following output to the console:

swift

```
["Monday", "Tuesday", "Wednesday", "Thursday", "Friday", "Saturday",
"Sunday"]
```

While iterating over enumerations is one aspect of defining data structures, it's also important to look at how protocols are used in Swift.

Protocols and Protocol-Oriented Programming

Protocols define a set of methods, properties, and requirements that a type must conform to. They serve as blueprints, establishing a contract for communication and behavior between different types. Protocol-oriented programming (POP) is a paradigm that emphasizes the use of protocols to define behavior and enable code reuse. It encourages composition and protocol conformance over traditional class-based inheritance. By focusing on protocols, POP promotes modular and extensible code, allowing for greater flexibility and scalability.

POP allows for reusable code and encourages composing types using protocols rather than relying solely on class hierarchies. This approach allows for flexible combinations of behaviors through protocol conformance, enabling code to adapt and evolve easily. Protocols also facilitate unit testing and mocking by providing clear boundaries and contract-based interactions. With POP, it becomes easier to isolate and test individual components, leading to more robust and maintainable code. Protocol extensions and default implementations provide a mechanism for adding new functionality to existing types without modifying their original implementation.

When adopting protocol-oriented programming, there are a few things to consider. Try to use protocols over inheritance: protocol conformance can achieve code reuse and composition. Try to compose multiple protocols together to create complex behaviors. This approach allows for fine-grained control over functionality and promotes modular design. Protocol extensions can provide default implementations and shared functionality. This reduces code duplication and improves maintainability. Finally, value types (structs and enums) align well with protocol-oriented programming principles, as they promote immutability, thread safety, and value semantics.

Implementing Protocols and Conforming to Them

Protocols enable developers to define common behavior and establish communication between different types. Protocols serve as blueprints, defining a set of methods, properties, and requirements that a type must adhere to. They establish a contract, ensuring that conforming types implement the specified functionality. By adopting protocols, we can achieve code reuse, enhance modularity, and facilitate polymorphism.

To implement a protocol, a type must conform to it by providing implementations for all the required methods, properties, and other requirements defined within the protocol. This enables the type to fulfill the contract established by the protocol.

Defining a Conforming Type

When creating a new type that conforms to a protocol, declare its conformance by listing the protocol name after the type's declaration, separated by a colon. For example, if we have a protocol named `MyProtocol`, a class conforming to it would be declared as follows:

swift

```
class MyClass: MyProtocol {
    // Implement required methods and properties here
}
```

Protocol requirements can include both instance and static methods, properties, initializers, and associated types. When conforming to a protocol, we need to provide implementations for all required requirements.

To implement an instance method or property from a protocol, we define it within the conforming type and provide the necessary implementation. Ensure that the method or property signature matches the protocol requirement. Similar to instance methods and properties, type methods and properties defined in a protocol can also be implemented by conforming types. For requirements declared with `static`, structs and enums use `static`; classes can use either `static` or `class`, depending on whether overriding is desired.

Conforming types have the flexibility to provide additional functionality beyond the protocol requirements. They can implement their own methods and properties as well as conform to multiple protocols simultaneously, which allows for customization and tailoring of behavior to suit specific needs.

Delegation with Protocols

Delegation is a design pattern that allows one object to delegate certain tasks to another object. This helps decouple code to make it more reusable and helps to avoid writing repetitive code. One way to implement delegation is to use protocols. As a blueprint for a type, protocols define a set of methods, properties, and other requirements that a type must conform to in order to adopt the protocol.

To implement delegation using protocols, first define a protocol that declares the tasks the delegating object wants to hand off. The protocol should define a method for each task. Once the protocol is defined, the delegate type adopts the protocol and implements those methods.

Finally, the delegating object stores a reference to the delegate and calls the delegate's protocol methods when needed. The following example shows how to implement delegation using protocols:

swift

```
protocol Profile: AnyObject {
  func install()
}
class PasswordProfile: Profile {
  func install() {
    print("Installing the password profile")
  }
}
class ViewController: UIViewController {
  weak var delegate: Profile?
  @IBAction func installProfile(_ sender: Any) {
    delegate?.install()
  }
}
```

In this example, the `ViewController` class uses a delegate property of type `Profile?`. That means it can be `nil` or can store an instance of a type that conforms to the `Profile` protocol. The `ViewController` class also has an `installProfile()` action method. This method calls `install()` on the delegate property. If the delegate property is `nil`, the method does nothing.

To use the `ViewController` class, you would first create an instance of a type that conforms to the `Profile` protocol. For example, you could create a `PasswordProfile` instance. Next, you would assign the `PasswordProfile` instance to the delegate property on the `ViewController` instance. You could then call the `installProfile()` method on the `ViewController` instance. This would cause the `ViewController` instance to call the `install()` method on the `PasswordProfile` instance.

Conditional Conformance

Conditional conformance allows types to conform to a protocol only when certain conditions are met. This makes code more flexible and reusable, helps avoid repetitive code, and makes code more type-safe. To implement conditional conformance, add a `where` clause to the conformance declaration. For example:

swift

```
struct Box<Value> {
  let value: Value
}
extension Box: Equatable where Value: Equatable {}
```

This means Box conforms to Equatable only when the wrapped Value type also conforms to Equatable. The following example shows how to use this conditional conformance:

swift

```
let a = Box(value: 8)
let b = Box(value: 8)
print(a == b) // true
```

In this example, a and b can be compared for equality because Int conforms to Equatable. Conditional conformance helps keep generic code type-safe by only enabling protocol behavior when the generic constraints are satisfied.

Protocols support inheritance, enabling the creation of protocol hierarchies. A protocol can inherit one or more protocols, thereby inheriting their requirements. By conforming to a protocol that inherits from others, a type automatically inherits the requirements of all the inherited protocols. By adhering to protocol contracts, types can communicate and share behavior, promoting code reuse, flexibility, and enhanced modularity.

Make Protocol Requirements Optional

There is one way to make a protocol requirement truly optional in Swift: use the @objc attribute with the optional keyword. This method is compatible with Objective-C and can only be used with class types. A different pattern is to use a protocol extension to provide a default implementation. That does not make the requirement optional, but it allows conforming types to reuse shared behavior.

To use @objc and optional, add @objc to the protocol and optional to the requirement. For example, the following code shows a protocol with an optional requirement:

swift

```
@objc protocol Animal {
  @objc optional func speak()
}
```

Any class that conforms to the `Animal` protocol can now choose to implement the `speak()` method or not. To provide shared default behavior with protocol extensions, create an extension and define a default implementation for the requirement. For example:

swift

```
protocol Animal {
  func speak()
}
extension Animal {
  func speak() {
    print("Animal noise")
  }
}
```

Now, any type that conforms to the `Animal` protocol will have a default implementation of the `speak()` method, unless it chooses to provide its own implementation.

The method you choose depends on your specific needs. If you need truly optional protocol requirements with Objective-C interoperability, use `@objc optional`. If you need cross-type shared behavior for classes, structs, and enums, use protocol extensions with default implementations.

Protocol Extensions and Default Implementations

Protocols play a vital role in defining common behavior and establishing communication between different types as projects grow. They allow for code reuse and provide a blueprint for structuring our codebase. Protocols then enhance the flexibility and expressiveness of our code.

Understanding Protocols

Protocols in Swift serve as a way to define a set of methods, properties, and requirements that a type must conform to. They establish a contract, enabling different types to adhere to a common interface. By adopting protocols, we can achieve greater modularity, abstraction, and maintainability in our code.

Protocol extensions enable us to provide default implementations for methods, properties, and other requirements defined in protocols. This feature allows us to extend the functionality of existing types that conform to a protocol without modifying their original implementation. By defining default implementations within a protocol extension, we can avoid duplicating code across multiple conforming types. Furthermore, protocol extensions improve code in a few ways.

Protocol extensions make code even more reusable and flexible and promote composition over inheritance. Protocol extensions allow us to share common functionality across multiple types. We can provide default implementations for methods or properties, reducing code duplication and improving maintainability. With protocol extensions, we can extend the behavior of existing types, including classes, structs, and enums, without subclassing or modifying their original implementation. This enables us to add new functionality to types that we don't control. Protocol extensions encourage the use of composition-based approaches instead of relying solely on inheritance. By defining protocols and extending them, we can compose different behaviors and achieve more flexible code structures.

Default implementations complement protocol extensions by providing a default implementation for a method or property in a protocol extension. By defining default implementations in protocol extensions, it's possible to ensure that all conforming types have access to the same default behavior.

Protocol Property and Method Requirements

Protocols are blueprints for defining the behavior of a type. They can be used to specify the properties and methods that a type must implement. To define a protocol property requirement, use the `var` keyword with getter/setter requirements. As an example, the following code defines a protocol with a property requirement to check for the presence of antivirus software on a device:

swift

```
protocol Antivirus {
  var name: String { get }
}
```

Any class, struct, or enum that conforms to the Antivirus protocol must implement the name property. To define a protocol method requirement, use the `func` keyword followed by the method name, parameters, and return type. For example, the following code defines a protocol with a method requirement:

swift

```
protocol Antivirus {
  func get()
}
```

Any class, struct, or enum that conforms to the Antivirus protocol must implement the `get()` method. This logic can also be extended to class hierarchies with required initializers.

Initializer Requirements

Required initializers are used to ensure that all subclasses of a class implement a specific initializer. Doing so helps ensure that subclasses are initialized correctly. It also provides a common initializer for all subclasses and forces them to implement a specific initializer required by the superclass. To define a required initializer, use the `required` keyword before the initializer declaration. For example, the following code defines a required initializer for the `Bind` class used to bind to a directory service:

swift

```
class Bind {
  required init(name: String) {
    self.name = name
  }
  var name: String
}
```

This means that all subclasses of the Bind class must implement an initializer with the same signature as the required initializer. The following example shows how to use an initializer requirement:

swift

```
class Bind {
  required init(name: String) {
    self.name = name
  }
  var name: String
}
class ActiveDirectory: Bind {
  var cert: String = ""

  required init(name: String) {
    super.init(name: name)
  }

  init(name: String, cert: String) {
    self.cert = cert
    super.init(name: name)
  }
}
let activedirectory = ActiveDirectory(name: "charles", cert: "0x001")
print(activedirectory.name) // Prints "charles"
print(activedirectory.cert) // Prints "0x001"
```

In this example, the ActiveDirectory class subclasses the Bind class and implements the required initializer. This means that ActiveDirectory objects can be created and initialized correctly.

Initializer requirements can help to force subclasses to implement a specific initializer that is required by the superclass. This can help to encapsulate the implementation of the initializer and prevent subclasses from breaking the superclass's implementation. When using initializer requirements, be careful not to make code too inflexible. Requiring subclasses to implement too many initializers can make code difficult to extend and maintain.

Conforming Types and Overriding

When a type conforms to a protocol that includes default implementations, it has the option to either use the default implementation as is or override it with its own implementation. This gives the conforming type the flexibility to customize the default behavior based on its specific requirements.

Preventing Overriding

The `final` keyword prevents a class, method, or property from being overridden. This can be useful for preventing unwanted changes to code in a polymorphic world. To use the `final` keyword, add it to the declaration of the class, method, or property to prevent it from being overridden. For example:

swift

```
class MyClass {
    // This method cannot be overridden
    final func myMethod() {}
}
```

The `final` keyword can also be used to prevent a class from being subclassed by adding `final` to the class declaration. For example:

swift

```
final class MyClass {}
```

Classes that are declared final cannot be subclassed. This can be useful for preventing unwanted changes to code.

Protocols As Types

Protocols can be used as types in a number of ways. For example, you can use a protocol as the type of

- A variable or constant
- A parameter to a function
- A return value from a function
- An element in an array, dictionary, or other collection

When using protocols as types, it is important to choose descriptive names for protocols. This will help other developers understand what the protocol is for and how to use it. Also, document protocols clearly. This will help other developers understand what the protocol requires and how to conform to it.

The `protocol` keyword is used to define a protocol. The following example shows a protocol used as a type:

swift

```
protocol Extensions {
  func showList()
}
class FirefoxExtensions: Extensions {
  func showList() {
    print("Here is a list of all installed Firefox extensions")
  }
}
class NetworkExtensions: Extensions {
  func showList() {
    print("Here is a list of all installed Network extensions")
  }
}
// Declare a variable of an existential protocol type.
var extensions: any Extensions
// Assign a FirefoxExtensions object to the variable.
extensions = FirefoxExtensions()
// Call the showList() method on the variable.
extensions.showList() // Prints "Here is a list of all installed Firefox
extensions"
// Reassign a NetworkExtensions object to the variable.
extensions = NetworkExtensions()
// Call the showList() method on the variable.
extensions.showList() // Prints "Here is a list of all installed Network
extensions"
```

In this example, the Extensions protocol is used as the type of the extensions variable. This means that any type that conforms to the Extensions protocol can be assigned to the variable.

Type Constraints and Protocol Extensions

Protocol extensions can also be constrained to specific types, allowing us to extend only those types that meet certain criteria. This capability is useful when we want to add functionality to a subset of types that conform to a protocol, providing more specialized behavior for those types.

Protocol extensions and default implementations provide a powerful mechanism for extending the behavior of types that conform to protocols. They promote code reuse, enhance modularity, and enable flexible composition-based designs. By leveraging these features, Swift developers can write cleaner, more maintainable code while enjoying the benefits of a robust and expressive programming language.

Actors

Actors are a concurrency primitive introduced in Swift 5.5. They are designed to provide a safe way to manage concurrent access to mutable state in code. Actors are reference types, which means that they can be passed around and shared between different parts of your code. Actor-isolated state is protected so that actor-isolated code on a given actor runs serially.

Actors work with Swift's async/await concurrency model. If you are new to concurrency, you may also encounter other tools such as Grand Central Dispatch (GCD) or `OperationQueue`. To use actors, use the `actor` keyword. For example:

swift

```
actor MyActor {
    func doSomething() {
        // This code runs in actor isolation
    }
}
```

Once you have created an actor, you can create instances of it. For example:

swift

```
let myActor = MyActor()
```

You can then call methods on the actor using `await`. For example:

swift

```
Task {
    await myActor.doSomething()
}
```

When calling a method on an actor from outside that actor, the method is executed in actor isolation. Access to actor-isolated state is serialized, though async actor methods can still interleave at suspension points. Here is an example of how to use actors to implement a simple concurrent counter:

swift

```
actor Counter {
    private var count = 0
    func increment() {
        count += 1
    }
    func decrement() {
        count -= 1
    }
    func getCount() -> Int {
        return count
    }
}
let counter = Counter()
Task {
    // Increment the counter
    await counter.increment()
    // Decrement the counter
```

```
    await counter.decrement()
    // Get the current count
    let count = await counter.getCount()
    print(count)
}
```

This code increments the counter, decrements the counter, and then gets the current count. Each actor method call is isolated, but the full sequence is not one atomic transaction. For more information on actors, refer to the actors documentation: `https://developer.apple.com/documentation/swift/actor`.

Index

A

B

C

C. Edge et al., *Mastering Swift*, https://doi.org/10.1007/979-8-8688-2770-9

D

E

F

N

O

P, Q

R

GPSR Compliance
The European Union's (EU) General Product Safety Regulation (GPSR) is a set of rules that requires consumer products to be safe and our obligations to ensure this.

If you have any concerns about our products, you can contact us on

ProductSafety@springernature.com

In case Publisher is established outside the EU, the EU authorized representative is:

Springer Nature Customer Service Center GmbH
Europaplatz 3
69115 Heidelberg, Germany

www.ingramcontent.com/pod-product-compliance
Lightning Source LLC
Chambersburg PA
CBHW080255250826
50385CB00022B/614
9798868827693